Democracy, Education, and Equality

Many believe that equality of opportunity will be achieved when the prospects of children no longer depend upon the wealth and education of their parents. The institution through which the link between child and parental prospects may be weakened is public education. Many also believe that democracy is the political institution that will bring about justice. This publication asks whether democracy, modeled as competition between political parties that represent different interests in the polity, will result in educational funding policies that will, at least eventually, produce citizens who have equal capacities (human capital), thus breaking the link between family background and child prospects. In other words, will democracy engender, through the educational finance policies it produces, a state of equal opportunity in the long run? Several models of the problem are studied, which vary according to the educational technology posited, that is, the relationship between family inputs, school inputs, and the eventual human capital of the adult the child becomes. The main innovation of the publication is to model political competition between parties as ruthless. The policies that parties may choose lie in a very large policy space: they need be of any parametric functional form. Equilibrium in the game of party competition is a variant of the author's "party-unanimity Nash equilibrium," or PUNE.

John E. Roemer is the Elizabeth S. and A. Varick Stout Professor of Political Science and Economics at Yale University. He has published extensively in economics, political philosophy, and political science. His recent books include *Political Competition* (2001), *Equality of Opportunity* (1998), *Theories of Distributive Justice* (1996), and *A Future for Socialism* (1994). He was elected a Fellow of the Econometric Society in 1986 and a Corresponding Fellow of the British Academy in 2005.

Econometric Society Monographs No. 40

Editors:

Andrew Chesher, University College London
Matthew Jackson, California Institute of Technology

The Econometric Society is an international society for the advancement of economic theory in relation to statistics and mathematics. The Econometric Society Monograph Series is designed to promote the publication of original research contributions of high quality in mathematical economics and theoretical and applied econometrics.

Other titles in the series:

Continued on page following the index

Democracy, Education, and Equality

Graz-Schumpeter Lectures

John E. Roemer
Yale University

CAMBRIDGE
UNIVERSITY PRESS

CAMBRIDGE UNIVERSITY PRESS
Cambridge, New York, Melbourne, Madrid, Cape Town, Singapore, São Paulo

Cambridge University Press
40 West 20th Street, New York, NY 10011-4211, USA

www.cambridge.org
Information on this title: www.cambridge.org/9780521846653

First published 2006

Printed in the United States of America

A catalog record for this publication is available from the British Library.

Library of Congress Cataloging in Publication Data

Roemer, John E.
Democracy, education, and equality / John E. Roemer.
   p.   cm. – (Econometric Society monographs ; no. 40)
Includes bibliographical references and index.
ISBN-13: 978-0-521-84665-3 (hardback)
ISBN-10: 0-521-84665-X (hardback)
ISBN-13: 978-0-521-60913-5 (pbk.)
ISBN-10: 0-521-60913-5 (pbk.)
1. Politics and education – Econometric models.   2. Democracy – Economic aspects.
3. Educational equalization – Econometric models.   4. Social choice – Econometric
models.   5. Human capital – Econometric models.   6. Government aid to
education – Econometric models.   7. Equality – Econometric models.
I. Title.   II. Series.
LC71.R64   2005
379.2'6 – dc22   2005019575

ISBN-13   978-0-521-84665-3 hardback
ISBN-10   0-521-84665-X hardback

ISBN-13   978-0-521-60913-5 paperback
ISBN-10   0-521-60913-5 paperback

Contents

Acknowledgments

I began working on this topic five years ago, with Ignacio Ortuño-Ortin of the University of Alicante. Due to the physical distance between us, we eventually diverged into working separately on the problem. I am indebted to him for many early discussions, and, indeed, very possibly, for the initial formulation of the problem.

Roger E. Howe and I spent hours working on some of the mathematical problems that arose. In particular, Theorem 4.2, on dynamics, is a collaboration. I owe a great deal to Roger, who has been my loyal mathematical consultant for some thirty years.

Herbert Scarf showed me an elementary technique for verifying solutions to concave optimization problems on infinite dimensional spaces that I use throughout the analysis.

John Geanakoplos, Joaquim Silvestre, Colin Stewart, Karine Van der Straeten, Juan D. Moreno-Ternero, and Cong Huang read versions of this work, more or less in that order over a period of years, and made important criticisms and suggestions. Joseph Altonji advised me on the econometric estimation in Chapter 6. I did not check all the details with him, so he is not responsible for any errors committed. I also received valuable advice on the appropriate data sets to use for the estimation in Chapter 6 from Carolyn Hoxby. My research assistant, Thomas Pepinsky, performed the data analysis and econometric estimation in that chapter. In the later stages, I had useful mathematical discussions with David Pollard and Cong Huang. Cong receives the credit for writing a computer program to carry out the dynamic simulation in Chapter 4, section E in real time. Finally, Matthew Jackson, as editor of the Econometric Society Monographs Series in which this volume appears, made helpful stylistic suggestions. I am grateful to all of these generous colleagues and students.

This material was first presented as the Graz Schumpeter Lectures at the University of Graz in May 2003. I am extremely grateful to the Graz Schumpeter Society for that invitation. Professor Stefan Boehm, the Society's chairperson at the time, extended a most gracious welcome, and the lectures were a stimulating occasion, perfectly complemented by a weekend visit to the Styrian wine country. I believe the lectures fit properly within the scope of Joseph Schumpeter's interests, although that criterion may be too easily fulfilled, given Schumpeter's intellectual breadth.

JER
Yale University
March 2005

CHAPTER 1

A Brief Overview

The conception of social justice held by many, perhaps most, citizens of the Western democracies is that of equality of opportunity. Exactly what that kind of equality requires is a contested issue, but many would refer to the metaphor of 'leveling the playing field,' or setting the initial conditions in the competition for social goods so as to give all, regardless of their backgrounds, an equal chance at achievement. A central institution to implement that field leveling is education, meaning education that is either publicly financed or made available to all at affordable costs. Currently the political institution of choice is democracy, which is implemented by competitive political parties, ones that may freely form and enter that competition, representing different interest groups in the polity.

It is thus incumbent upon a social scientist who is concerned with inequality to ask: Will democracy succeed in organizing political competition around the issue of public education, so as to implement, over time, policies that will engender equality of opportunity? This publication asks whether the central contemporary measure of *social justice* will be achieved through the main contemporary *political mechanism* through its manner of financing the *educational institution*.

The two main sources within a country of inequality of opportunity are the different family backgrounds from which children come, and their differential native abilities. Here I wish to concentrate upon social inequalities, and so in the models that I examine, it is assumed that all children have the same native talent. Differences in the achievements of children when they become adults will be due solely to two factors:

1

their different family backgrounds, and the quality of education that they enjoy (which will have been publicly funded through taxation). To be more precise, I will address the formation of human capital, or income-earning capacity, in children through educational investment.

The data for the models that I study must specify the following: the distribution of endowments of families, the technology of education, the preferences of citizen-voters, the institutions of political competition, and the concept of political equilibrium.

A family will consist of an adult and a child, and it will be characterized by the *level of human capital*, or wage-earning capacity, of its adult member. That is its sole endowment. Thus, a society at any given date is characterized by a distribution of human capital of its adult members. It will be assumed that each adult cares about two quantities: the consumption level of the family and the future human capital of his or her child when he or she has finished the educational process and becomes an adult. In particular, adults do not value leisure, and so it will be assumed that every adult produces a fixed income, independent of what taxation will be imposed, equal to the adult's level of human capital. We will in fact assume that adults have simple, Cobb-Douglas preferences over these two quantities, consumption and the future human capital of the child.

We will study two different educational technologies. First, we postulate that the level of human capital a child will come to have is an increasing function of two variables: his parent's level of human capital and the amount invested in his education. We think of the influence of parental human capital as occurring through 'family culture,' something that we do not model in any more detail. With this first technology, the earning capacity of a child is thus determined entirely locally – by family background and investment in the child. (Later, we will examine a technology in which there are external [global] effects.) Because of the influence of family culture on the future earning capacity of the child, if one wished to equalize the earning capacities of children from different families, more would have to be invested in the education of children from poorer families. We take an optimistic view, that such equality of outcomes could always be achieved with a sufficiently large investment in the education of the more disadvantaged child. In particular, we will assume that the educational technology is also of the Cobb-Douglas form, with respect to the two inputs of parental human capital and educational investment; it is given by

$$h' = \alpha h^b r^c,$$

where h is the human capital of the parent, r is the educational investment in the child, and h' is the level of human capital the child will come to possess.

The political institution that we model is party competition, where parties form endogenously to represent the two elements of a partition of the polity. Indeed, we assume that there will be only two parties, one representing all those citizens whose human capital is below some value, and the other, all other citizens. Thus, democracy is modeled as a competition between the (relatively) poor and the (relatively) rich. Parties compete over the size of the budget used to fund education, the allocation of that budget to the education of children classified by their 'type,' that is, the human capital of their family, and the redistribution of post-tax income among families.

The main innovation of this publication is its attempt to model political competition as 'ruthless,' or having very few restrictions on the proposals that parties can make with regard to these policies. Denote by h the human capital of the adult in a family, and suppose that the support of the distribution of human capital, at the date in question, is the positive real line, and that h is distributed according to a probability measure F whose mean is μ. Then a policy will consist of two functions, $r : \mathbb{R}_+ \to \mathbb{R}_+$ and $\psi : \mathbb{R}_+ \to \mathbb{R}_+$ where $r(h)$ is the amount to be invested in the child from an h family, and $\psi(h)$ is the after-tax income of an h family. The sole restrictions on these functions is that they be continuous and satisfy:

$$\int X(h)dF(h) = \mu \tag{1.1}$$

$$0 \leq X'(h) \leq 1 \tag{1.2}$$

where $X(h) \equiv r(h) + \psi(h)$. Equation (1.1) is the society's budget constraint, and Equation (1.2) puts restrictions on the upper and lower bounds of the derivative of the 'total resource bundle' going to families, when these derivatives exist. Thus, parties are not restricted to choose affine consumption or investment policies, or indeed policies restricted to be of any parametric form.

We adopt this approach of working on a very large policy space (one which is infinite dimensional) in order to model the idea that there are no holds barred in the competition between citizen coalitions represented by parties, except those stated by the continuity of these policy functions, and the limitations on the derivatives of Equation (1.2). We do this because our interest is in examining *democracy*, and that examination would be truncated if artificial restrictions were to be placed on democratic competition. Indeed, what emerges from our analysis is that the policies proposed by parties in equilibrium are *piece-wise linear* ones, and this accords very well with reality because tax policies in almost all advanced democracies are, indeed, piece-wise linear.

The conceptual problem that we face is to propose a theory of political equilibrium in which equilibria will exist, when parties do compete on such large policy spaces. The classical model of political competition (due to Harold Hotelling and Anthony Downs) only possesses equilibria for two-party competition when the policy space is *uni*dimensional. So something else is needed. Here, we use a modified version of the *party-unanimity Nash equilibrium* that I introduced in earlier work (see Roemer, 1999, 2001). This equilibrium concept is introduced in Chapter 2. Parties are modeled as consisting of factions that bargain with each other in the face of competition from the other party. The factions represent the conflict between those who wish to use the party as a vehicle to winning power (the 'Opportunists') and those who view it as an instrument for representing constituency interests (the Reformists and Militants, or Guardians). An equilibrium is, roughly speaking, a pair of policies – one for each party – each of which is a solution of the bargaining problem facing the factions in one party, *given* the policy being proposed by the other party. Indeed, this equilibrium concept uses two ideas of John Nash – his bargaining solution and his non-cooperative equilibrium concept.

The fortuitous result is that, because of the divided interests of those who formulate party policy (that is, the various factions), equilibria exist in the party-competition game, even though the policy space is very large. Thus, our approach 'solves' the problem afflicting the

Hotelling-Downs model of the non-existence of equilibrium for multi-dimensional policy spaces. Indeed, there are *many* equilibria of our model – too many, one might say – a two-dimensional set (or manifold) of them. Each equilibrium is associated with a different pair of numbers that summarize the relative strengths of the bargaining factions in the two parties. Thus, we may view the model's missing data as the relative bargaining powers of the internal party factions. How we deal with this multiplicity of equilibria will be described below.

Let us suppose, for the moment, that we can single out a unique equilibrium at a certain date, given the data of the problem, which consist of the distribution of human capital across families (their adults), adult preferences over policies, and the technology of education. We can then state our full problem as follows. Suppose that time begins, at date zero, with an initial distribution of human capital, F^0. Parties form, and an equilibrium in the party-competition game exists – by supposition, we have chosen one uniquely. According to the model, one party wins the election, but this is a stochastic event because the equilibrium concept only specifies the probability that each of the two parties wins the election. The victorious party implements its policy, including, in particular, its policy of education finance. Thus, for example, if the Poor and Rich parties proposed equilibrium policies (r^P, ψ^P) and (r^R, ψ^R) and party P wins, then it implements its educational finance policy, which means it invests, after taxation, amount $r^P(h)$ in every child from an h-human capital family, and this for every h.

Chapter 3 is devoted to the definition and characterization of the set of equilibria of the political model at a single date. This is where it is shown that, in equilibrium, parties always propose piece-wise linear functions for the policy components.

Once we have specified a particular educational finance policy, then, via the educational technology, we have determined (with no random element) the human capital of every child when he or she becomes an adult. Thus, the distribution of human capital at date one is determined, call it F^1, subject only to the stochastic element of which party wins the election. Now the same model tells us what happens at date one. Parties form, an equilibrium in policies occurs, which determines (subject to the stochastic election element) a winner, and hence the distribution of human capital at date two, F^2.

We now assume that this process continues for a very long time. This is a 'stochastic dynamic' process, leading to an infinite sequence of distributions of human capital: F^1, F^2, F^3.... Our question is: What happens to the degree of inequality of human capital over time? Does this sequence converge to an 'equal' distribution of human capital, or not? Does democracy eliminate the inequality associated with the different social backgrounds from which members of these dynasties come? This is the topic of Chapter 4.

We measure the degree of inequality in a distribution by its coefficient of variation, the standard deviation divided by the mean. Thus, if the coefficients of variation of the sequence $\{F^t\}$ approach zero as a limit, we say that democracy engenders equality in the long run. Indeed, we are interested in what happens to the ratios of human capital in any two dynasties. If these ratios *all* converge to unity, then equality of opportunity holds in the long run, in the sense that the imprint of the family background upon the human capital of future members of any dynasty eventually disappears.

Here I avoid the question of how we choose, at each date, a unique equilibrium from among the large set of equilibria that exist. I must be more specific at this point. One way of specifying a particular equilibrium is to specify where the *pivot* lies, which separates the polity into the poor and rich, and into the two parties, and once that is done, to specify the degree of *opportunism* or *partisanship* that characterizes the political competition. To study the dynamical question, I examine two intertemporal sequences of equilibria. In both sequences I fix the pivot at each date to belong to a single dynasty – for example, the dynasty that has the median value of human capital at all dates. I must remark that, in these dynamic processes, the rank of any given dynasty in the distribution of human capital remains fixed forever. Thus, if Smith occupies the median rank of human capital at date zero, then in all equilibria of the model, all of Smith's descendents will also occupy the median rank. Because children are modeled as all having the same internal talent, rank-switching over time never occurs in this model.

Having fixed a rank to characterize the pivot dynasty, I now examine two sequences of equilibria, which I call A and B. In the A sequence political competition is as opportunistic as it possibly can be, and in the B sequence it is as partisan as it possibly can be. That is, in A, the Opportunists are the ones who dominate in intra-party bargaining, and in B, the Militants or Guardians dominate in the bargaining. Indeed, in A, it turns out that at every date, both parties propose the same policy in equilibrium, that policy which is the ideal policy of the pivot voter. In B, parties propose policies that are different – indeed, as different as they ever will be in equilibrium.

It turns out that in both the A and B sequences, the coefficients of variation decrease monotonically over time. At least we can say that democracy has an equalizing effect on the distribution of human capital. But the results beyond this are quite different. In the A sequence, we prove that the limit coefficient of variation is always positive, that is, democratic competition will never entirely eliminate inequality of opportunity.

Analysis of the B sequence is more difficult; I do not have complete analytical results. However, simulations are useful, and indicate that the following is true: if the initial distribution F^0 is sufficiently skewed, then there is a *positive probability* that the limit coefficient of variation of the dynamic sequence is zero. If the initial distribution is not sufficiently skewed, then we prove that the coefficient of variation surely converges to a positive number. Indeed, strongly skewed means precisely the following: at date zero, if h^* is the human capital of the pivot, then the following is true:

$$\log h^* < \int \log h \, dF^0(h).$$

In sum, there is never a guarantee that democracy will engender equality of opportunity in the long run. The most we can say is that such an outcome will occur with positive probability if two conditions hold: that (1) political competition is sufficiently partisan as opposed to opportunist, and that (2) the initial distribution of human capital is 'strongly skewed.'

Analysis of the problem with the large policy space described here is difficult, relatively speaking, and so it is worthwhile to ask how different the result would be if we restricted competition to occurring on a unidimensional policy space, and used the classical Hotelling-Downs model of equilibrium, where both parties propose the ideal policy of the voter with median human capital. It turns out that this analysis is quite simple (see Chapter 4). The theorem is: If the original distribution of human capital is strongly skewed (in exactly the above sense), then the coefficient of variation converges to zero. If it is not strongly skewed, then it converges to a positive number.

Thus, the Downsian model supports a starker, less subtle result than the model of 'ruthless competition.' Downsian competition is of the opportunist kind: both political parties are completely dominated by opportunists in the sense that parties do not represent constituents at all, but desire only to maximize the probability of winning the election. With the unidimensional policy space and Downsian politics, we have that, with initial strong skewness, political competition always leads to equality in the long run, while in the model of ruthless competition, opportunist politics *never* leads to equality in the long run. Moreover, even with *partisan* competition in the model with the large policy space, convergence to equality is never a sure event, but it occurs with positive probability with initial strong skewness. We conclude that the Downsian model provides a misleading prediction of the nature of democratic politics – and this, if anything, justifies our study.

These results are somewhat pessimistic if one harbored the thought that democracy would, at least in the long run, eliminate differentials in human capacity due to family influence. In Chapter 5 we study what happens over time to inequality if the educational technology is of the form

$$h' = \alpha h^b r^c \bar{r}^d, \qquad (1.3)$$

where $\bar{r}$ is the average educational investment in the entire cohort of children. With this technology, we have an external effect: a child's human capital is determined not only by what is invested in him or her, but what is invested in all children. This can also be called a model of endogenous growth.

There are several interpretations of the process that would engender this kind of technology. One is that children learn from each other, so there are positive external economies to increasing average investment. A second is that technological change is fostered by increasing total investment, which raises wages, which, in our model, are the same as human capital.

Intuitively, the larger is the elasticity d and the smaller is the elasticity c in (1.3), the more voters have an interest in large investments in education on average, and the less they will care about how much is invested in their own children. What we show in Chapter 5 is a rigorous version of this intuition: if the ratio d/c is sufficiently large, then, even in the opportunist political equilibria, the coefficient of variation of the dynamic sequence of human capitals converges to zero.

Chapter 6 is the sole empirical effort in this study. We attempt to measure the elasticities b, c, and d from US data. We derive quite precise estimates of b and c, but are unable to estimate d. We therefore cannot tell if the size of d/c is as large as is required for the convergence results of Chapter 5 to hold. Perhaps a researcher more econometrically astute than the present author could reach more definitive conclusions.

A footnote should be added at this point. In the analysis of Chapter 4, I assume that $b + c = 1$. We find, however, in Chapter 6, that $b + c < 1$. The justification of my assumption in Chapter 4 is that, when $b + c = 1$, technology *as such* will not cause the coefficient of variation of human capital to converge to zero. By this I mean the following: when $b + c = 1$, then in the absence of any redistributive state action, and when individual families finance privately the education of their children, the coefficient of variation will remain *constant* over time. However, when $b + c < 1$, even in this laissez-faire case, the coefficient of variation of human capital *will* converge to zero. Therefore, the assumption that $b + c = 1$ allows us to neatly separate the (economic) effect on convergence of *technology* from the (political) effect of *democracy*. It is the appropriate assumption for one who, like myself, is concerned with studying the effect of democracy on equality.

If one were to assume that $b + c < 1$ in the model, then one would have to ask the question: Under what circumstances will democracy cause the distribution of human capital to converge to equality *more rapidly* than it would under laissez-faire? Admittedly, this is an important question. It is presumably a more difficult question to answer than the one I have worked on, but one hopes that the results that I present are indicative of what the results would be in that empirically more realistic case.

Suppose that it turns out that, empirically, the ratio d/c is too small to induce convergence of the distribution of human capital to equality. Is there anything else we can say? I believe so. The assumption on voter preferences that I make throughout the study is one of self-interest: each voter is interested only in his or her own dynasty (present consumption and the human capital of his or her child). If voters were altruistic, in the sense of being interested in the children of other families, then that would act very much like the external effect in the technology (1.3) earlier. With sufficient altruism, it would therefore be the case that the convergence of human capital to equality would occur over the long run. This is not surprising.

Thus, we can summarize our results by saying that if voters are only locally altruistic (care only about their own children), and there are no external effects in the educational technology, then convergence of the distribution of human capital to equality (the achievement of equal opportunity in the long run) never occurs for sure, but only with positive probability, and that, indeed, only under special conditions on the initial degree of skewness and the nature of political competition. If, however, voters are either globally altruistic or there are substantial external effects in education, then democracy will eliminate inequality of opportunity based upon differential family backgrounds.

The final chapter presents a number of caveats concerning the analysis.

CHAPTER 2

Models of Party Competition

A. POLITICAL PARTIES

For millenia, different interest groups in society – primarily, according to one prominent view, different economic classes – have fought each other for control of the economic surplus. Democracy is one institution that organizes that struggle, and it has, according to Adam Przeworski [1999], one principal virtue: it minimizes bloodshed, for an aspect of democracy is the peaceful transition from one regime to its elected successor; as well with universal suffrage, it gives every citizen a voice in the action. Of course, both of these virtues are imperfectly implemented in actual democracies, but, to a first-order approximation, democracy dominates other forms of rule with respect to these two criteria.

In the modern period, since 1789, the democratic struggle has been organized primarily through political parties. There are exceptions: some Swiss cantons practiced direct democracy until quite recently, in which decisions are made by committees of the whole polity. The party form has, however, been almost ubiquitous. Parties historically have represented different interest groups in the polity. Sometimes parties are identified by the name of their interest group, such as the Labor Party or the Farmers' Party. Often, however, they are identified by an ideology, such as the Socialist or Christian Democratic Party. The appropriate general abstraction is to think of the polity as composed of a set of types of citizen, where a type identifies a particular interest group, and then to think of parties as representing sets or coalitions of types. In one important case, the types are workers and capitalists, and the parties are a Labor or Socialist Party and a Bourgeois Party. But the interests of citizens are not only economic, and if economic, they are not always so polarized as in the worker-capitalist story, and so parties in general are more complex than in this example. So, while elections have often been called the forum of the 'democratic class struggle,' that name is too narrow.[1] Frequently parties represent different ethnic or religious interest groups, or groups that have different views (preferences) over issues that are removed from economic concerns, such as racial integration or abortion.

Some contemporary researchers are concerned with why parties exist (see Aldrich [1995]). One immediately thinks of the parallel question of why firms exist, which has spawned an important literature and theory. There is no doubt that the study of why democratic politics is organized as party competition will lead to important insights, but it is not a topic that we address here.

It is, however, worth remarking on the *nature* of political parties in this publication. In recent years, a revisionist strand of literature has argued that parties are epiphenomena, in the sense of not having an important influence on legislative outcomes. Keith Krehbiel (1993), for example, argues that the behavior of US congress members, although highly correlated with their party membership, is only coincidentally so; what congress members really do is vote their preferences, and those usually coincide with party positions but not always so. What Krehbiel argues is that parties do not act as a disciplining device on their own legislative members. But this observation, I believe, is not relevant to the conception of political party in this publication, for here parties are *simply* coalitions of citizens with similar preferences. Our important assumption is that, for reasons not here modeled (perhaps Duverger's law), only two candidates may run in an election, and parties are the coalitions of citizens that coordinate to choose those representatives. Parties are weak; Krehbiel is arguing that parties are not strong, which is consistent with this statement.

---

[1] Lipset (1960) so characterized elections.

B. THE HOTELLING-DOWNS MODEL

Historians have written about political parties for a long time. The first formal model of democratic party competition was posed by Harold Hotteling in 1929, although Erik Lindahl (1919) had a less successful model before him.[2] Hotelling's model was later elaborated and popularized by Anthony Downs (1957). I will present that model here, but in a slightly different form from the original. In particular, I will embed the model in an environment with uncertainty concerning voter behavior.

The political environment consists of a set of voter types, H; a set of policy platforms, T; a distribution of voter types in the polity, denoted by a probability measure $\mathbf{F}$ on H; and a profile of utility functions $v : T \times H \to \mathbf{R}$, which represents the preferences of a type h voter on the policy space T. For the moment, it will suffice for v to represent ordinal preferences on T, although a little later, I will want to think of v as a von Neumann-Morgenstern utility function on lotteries of policies.

We will assume that there is, in addition, some uncertainty associated with elections. Thus, if the voters face the choice between a pair of policies, not every voter will necessarily vote according to his or her preference order, or perhaps there is uncertainty about which voters will actually go to the polls to vote.

Let t^1, t^2 be a pair of policies. The set of voters who prefer t^1 to t^2 is denoted

$$H(t^1, t^2) = \{h \mid v(t^1, h) > v(t^2, h)\}.$$

In a model with perfect perception and costless voting these voters and only these voters would vote for t^1 over t^2 (assuming that no voter is indifferent between the policies or, more precisely, that the set of indifferent voters is of $\mathbf{F}$-measure zero, and so indifferent voters do

---

[2] For a brief excursus on the history of the formal modeling of the interaction between the economy and politics, see Roemer (2005).

not matter[3]). Then the fraction of the vote going to policy t^1 would be $\mathbf{F}(H(t^1, t^2))$. But we now assume that there is some aggregate uncertainty in how people will vote, so that the true fraction of the vote for the first policy will be $\mathbf{F}(H(t^1, t^2)) + X$, where X is a random variable not depending on t^1, t^2 with a mean of, say, zero. For simplicity, we might take X to be uniformly distributed on an interval $[-\beta, +\beta]$. Thus, the probability that the first policy wins the election is

$$\pi(t^1, t^2) \equiv \left[\mathbf{F}(H(t^1, t^2)) + X > \frac{1}{2} \right] = \Pr \left[X > \frac{1}{2} - \mathbf{F}(H(t^1, t^2)) \right],$$

which is easily seen to be given by the following formula, for the case $t^1 \neq t^2$:

$$\pi(t^1, t^2) = \begin{cases} 1, & \text{if } \dfrac{1}{2} - \mathbf{F}(H(t^1, t^2)) \leq -\beta \\[2mm] 0, & \text{if } \dfrac{1}{2} - \mathbf{F}(H(t^1, t^2)) \geq \beta \\[2mm] \dfrac{1}{2} + \dfrac{\mathbf{F}(H(t^1, t^2)) - \dfrac{1}{2}}{2\beta}, & \text{otherwise} \end{cases} \tag{2.1}$$

For our purposes the probability of victory for policy t^1 is an increasing function of the fraction of voters who are *expected* to vote for that policy, if everyone voted according to his or her preferences. If $t^1 = t^2$, then we predict that one-half the voters will vote for each policy, and by the same reasoning as above, we deduce that the probability of victory for each policy is one-half.

One might think, because the media typically now report that their polls are accurate to 2 or 3 percent, that the kind of uncertainty I am discussing is unimportant. But the relevant uncertainty here is not what the polls announce a day or week before the election: it is the uncertainty that parties face when they publish their manifestos, which typically occurs some months before the election. Research shows (see Klingerman et al. [1994]) that parties adhere quite closely to the platforms they publish in these manifestos, and at the point of publication, there may be substantial uncertainty about voter behavior because

---

[3] Notation: $\mathbf{F}$ denotes a probability measure on the real line, F is its cumulative distribution function, and f is its density function.

parties do not know exactly what the electorate believes, how candidate personality will affect voters, what scandals may be exposed during the campaign, what shocks may occur that change the salience of certain issues, and so on. So in many elections, the probability of victory for each party may be substantially less than one at the relevant point in time.

It is worth saying that the kind of uncertainty modeled here is not described by supposing that there are many i.i.d. random variables, one describing the stochastic behavior for each voter. Suppose a scandal involving one candidate is revealed during a campaign. That will cause many voters to shift away from that candidate. The 'randomness' in voter behavior that causes party uncertainty is in general correlated across voters.

We have now specified all the data necessary to define the political environment: it is the tuple $\langle H, \mathbf{F}, T, v, \beta \rangle$: the set of voter types and its distribution, the policy space, voter preferences, and the number β that allows us to compute the probability that any policy will defeat another.

In the Hotelling-Downs model, it is assumed that there are two parties or candidates. Each party is concerned solely with winning the election: thus, each party wishes to maximize its probability of victory. To be precise, we have a game played between two players, both of which have the strategy space T, and whose payoff functions are:

$$P^1(t^1, t^2) = \pi(t^1, t^2)$$
$$P^2(t^1, t^2) = 1 - \pi(t^1, t^2).$$

We define a *Hotelling-Downs equilibrium* as a Nash equilibrium of this game.

Define a type's *ideal policy* as the policy that maximizes its utility; that is $\hat{t}^h = \arg\max_t v(t, h)$.

Suppose that the policy space T is a real interval. Then there will exist a median ideal policy: that is, a policy t^* such that at least one-half the voters have that policy or a smaller one as their ideal policy, and at least one-half the voters have that policy or a larger one as their ideal policy.

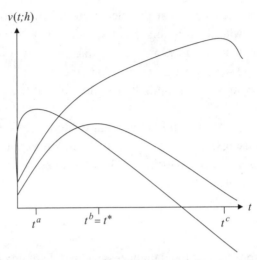

Figure 2.1. An illustration of the median-voter theorem.

We have: If T is an interval on the real line, and the utility functions $v(\cdot, h)$ are quasi-concave (in t), or – as the standard terminology puts it, *single-peaked*[4] in t – then there is a unique equilibrium: both parties play the median ideal policy, t^*.

Here is an example that illustrates the nature of the proof. In the example, there are three types whose utility functions are shown in Figure 2.1. The distribution of types is: 40 percent of the polity are type a, 30 percent are type b, and 30 percent are type c. The three ideal policies are marked on the t-axis; the median ideal policy is the ideal policy of type b. Let us check if there is a profitable deviation by either party from the policy pair (t^b, t^b). Were party 1 to play a policy $t^1 < t^b$, then party 2's predicted vote share is 70 percent, because both types b and c prefer t^b to t^1, which means that party 1 wins with lower probability than if it had not deviated. On the other hand, if party 1 deviates to $t^1 > t^b$ then its predicted vote share again becomes 30 percent, and its victory probability is less than if it had not deviated. Thus (t^b, t^b) is a Nash equilibrium of the game, and indeed the unique

---

[4] A function is *single-peaked* on a domain if it possesses exactly one local maximum, its global maximum.

Nash equilibrium. (For a rigorous version of the theorem in the general case, see Roemer [2001], Theorem 1.1, p. 21.)

Although I have defined a Hotelling-Downs equilibrium as a Nash equilibrium, this is a slightly anachronistic statement because Hotelling wrote before Nash. Hotelling probably had something like Nash equilibrium in mind. It is perhaps worth noting that, if there is certainty, and parties desire only to win (rather than to maximize vote share), then playing the ideal median policy is a dominant strategy equilibrium; the sophistication of the Nash concept is unneeded. In fact, Hotelling proposed a model with certainty.

The Hotelling-Downs model has had an immense influence in political science and modern political economy. Perhaps 95 percent of the papers that attempt to model politics formally employ this model of political competition, but it is an inadequate model of democratic politics. For if political competition is party competition, then the model misrepresents parties as being concerned only with winning elections. And if parties were interested only in winning elections, how could they possibly represent their constituencies, their interest groups? Interest groups do not care which *parties* hold power, but rather which *policies* get implemented.

In other words, a political party is the agent of its collective principal the set of voter types who, somehow, coalesce to form the party to fight for their interests. There is, indubitably, a principal-agent problem: the party may not perfectly represent its collective principal because politicians, the agents, have interests that diverge from the citizens whom they represent. Politicians want to remain in office, and that may induce them to undertake opportunist behavior – behavior that keeps them in office but is not in the interest of their principal. The Hotelling-Downs model represents politics as being completely dominated by these agents, who simply propose policies to maximize their chances of staying in office. This is an extreme view. If democracy is the institution through which different interest groups compete, an agency failure of a massive kind would be occurring if parties in general could thus escape their control.

To be somewhat more charitable, one might interpret the Hotelling-Downs model as one of parties that compete to gain office, because once in office, they can then implement policies favorable to their constituents. But in this case, the platforms that the parties propose in the model have nothing to do with what they will try to implement, and so voters must be assumed to be completely gullible and incapable of forming expectations about future party behavior. If parties had secret agendas, should not voters try to deduce them, and vote on the basis of those agendas, not the parties' platforms?

The Hotelling-Downs model was an invention of an economist. (Almost) nowhere in the historical literature do we find descriptions of parties that are Downsian, in the sense of being motivated *only* by the desire to maximize the probability of holding power. Mature parties, historically, have been almost always ideological: they wish to hold power gained by the promise to implement certain policies, which are in the interest of their constituencies or organizers. That the Hotelling-Downs model became so influential in formal political economy is due, I believe, to its being the *only* formal model of political competition for many years. Indeed, it was not until the mid-1970s that another model was presented.

C. THE WITTMAN-NASH MODEL

In 1973, Donald Wittman proposed a model of political competition where parties are partisan: they are assumed to have policy preferences. I will present a model based on Wittman's, although this one resolves certain problems that he did not face, and makes the representation aspect specific.[5] In Wittman's original presentation, party preferences are exogenous, and parties do not explicitly represent coalitions in the polity.

We have the same political environment as earlier, $\langle H, \mathbf{F}, T, v, \beta \rangle$. We now, however, think of the utility function v as representing von Neumann-Morgenstern preferences of the types, and, in addition, possessing cardinal unit comparability so that it is meaningful to add utilities across individuals.[6] I do not wish to endogenize the number

---

[5] This model first appeared in Roemer [2001, Chapter 5].

[6] It is, indeed, an interesting question whether it is reasonable to suppose that there exists a profile of vNM utility functions for a set of individuals that is also cardinally

of parties, which is a subtle undertaking; we suppose that exactly two parties will form. The two parties will each represent a coalition of voter types, thus, there will be a partition of the set of voter types

$$H = A \cup B, A \cap B = \emptyset,$$

with the parties called, also, A and B. Each party will represent its members, in the sense that the *party*'s preferences will be represented by a utility function that is the average of its members' utility functions; that is, we define the parties' utility functions on T by:

$$V^A(t) = \int_{h \in A} v(t, h) d\mathbf{F}(h),$$

$$V^B(t) = \int_{h \in B} v(t, h) d\mathbf{F}(h). \tag{2.2}$$

Each party is assumed to maximize the average expected utility of its members; thus, we define payoff functions for the two parties by:

$$Q^A(t^1, t^2) = \pi(t^1, t^2)V^A(t^1) + (1 - \pi(t^1, t^2))V^A(t^2),$$

$$Q^B(t^1, t^2) = \pi(t^1, t^2)V^B(t^1) + (1 - \pi(t^1, t^2))V^B(t^2). \tag{2.3}$$

We now have a game (T, Q^A, Q^B). We say that (t^A, t^B) is a *Wittman-Nash equilibrium for the environment* $\langle H, \mathbf{F}, T, v, \beta \rangle$ if

(1) (t^A, t^B) is a Nash equilibrium of the game (T, Q^A, Q^B), and
(2) for every $h \in A$, $v(t^A, h) \geq v(t^B, h)$, and for every $h \in B$, $v(t^B, h) \geq v(t^A, h)$.

Condition (1) is clear. Condition (2) says that the party structure is stable: no voter wishes to vote for the party of which he or she is not a member. Were (2) false, we imagine that discontented voters would switch parties; thus, (2) is the necessary condition of party stability.[7]

---

measurable and unit comparable, but one I will not pursue. For discussion of kinds of measurability and comparability of utility, see Roemer [1996, Chapter 1].

[7] We ignore the possibility that a set of strategically minded voters would join the opposition party in order to influence its preferences.

Here is an example. Suppose a voter's type is his or her income; thus, **F** is the distribution of income in society. We denote mean income by μ. The policy space is $T = [0,1]$, where t is a uniform proportional tax rate on income. Tax revenues are redistributed as a constant lump sum to all citizens. We assume that income is inelastically supplied, so at tax rate t, the after-tax income of a citizen h is

$$(1 - t)h + t\mu,$$

where μ is mean income. We assume that voters are risk neutral, and that the unit-comparable von Neumann-Morgenstern utility functions are

$$v(t, h) = (1 - t)h + t\mu = t(\mu - h) + h. \tag{2.4}$$

It is clear from examination of (2.4) that if $t^1 > t^2$, then the set of voter types who prefer the first policy is precisely the set whose income is less than μ; thus:

$$t^1 > t^2 \Rightarrow H(t^1, t^2) = \{h \mid h < \mu\}.$$

Consequently, from (2.1), the probability that the large tax rate defeats the smaller one is:

$$\pi(t^1, t^2) = \frac{1}{2} + \frac{F(\mu) - \frac{1}{2}}{2\beta} \equiv k, \tag{2.5}$$

a constant that is independent of the exact sizes of the two tax rates.

Now let $A = \{h < \mu\}$ and $B = \{h \geq \mu\}$. Then all members of A like large tax rates and all members of B, small tax rates. Indeed, the ideal policy of every member of A is $t = 1$, and the ideal policy of B's members is $t = 0$.

Now, as long as $t^1 > t^2$, using Equation (2.5), we can write the pay-off functions of the two parties as:

$$Q^A(t^1, t^2) = k(V^A(t^1) - V^A(t^2)) + V^A(t^2),$$
$$Q^B(t^1, t^2) = (1 - k)(V^B(t^2) - V^B(t^1)) + V^B(t^1).$$

Facing a policy t^2, party A must choose t^1 to maximize Q^A. Because k is constant, it is optimal to choose the uniform ideal policy of all its members, which is 1. In like manner, facing t^1, party B maximizes Q^B by choosing the uniform ideal policy of its members, which is 0. Indeed, this argument shows that each party has a dominant strategy in this example. So (1,0) is the unique Nash equilibrium of the game between these two parties. Finally, we see that each member of each party (weakly) prefers its party's policy to the opposition's, and so this is a Wittman equilibrium.

This example is extremely simple. It does not convey two important points: first, that in the general setting, the probability of a party's victory *does* depend on the policy it proposes, and second, that in general the equilibrium is not dominant-strategy. Because of this latter feature, we have called this concept the Wittman-*Nash* equilibrium. For examples of Wittman equilibrium that do display these two properties just referred to, see Roemer (2001, section 3.3, p. 55).

I have chosen this simple (non-representative) example because it suffices to show that the Wittman-Nash equilibrium gives a very different prediction from the Hotelling-Downs model: here, parties are completely polarized, whereas in Hotelling-Downs, they play the same policy. Generically, parties in Wittman equilibrium propose different policies. (See Roemer [2001, Chapter 3].) The policies are not always so extremely polarized – that is an artifact of this example, where the probability of victory is (relatively) unresponsive to policies. In most examples, there are more than two ideal policies in the set of voter types, probabilities of victory are responsive to policies, and as a consequence, parties are not so extreme. In those examples, as well, the equilibrium is not dominant strategy, but simply Nash.

If we believe that real parties propose different policies in equilibrium, then the Wittman-Nash model clearly captures the nature of political competition better than the Hotelling-Downs model. But more importantly, it is more intellectually satisfactory because it captures, albeit in a simple way, the idea that parties represent interest groups in the polity.

Of course, one might object that the principal-agent problem has ceased to exist in the Wittman model: parties perfectly represent their constituencies – opportunistic politicians play no role. A Wittmanesque party puts no value on office holding per se. We will address this issue in what follows.[8]

I have described the Downs-Hotelling and Wittman-Nash concepts in an environment of party uncertainty concerning voter behavior. But what happens in a world of certainty? Both equilibrium concepts produce convergent politics in which both parties play the median ideal policy. (For proof, see Roemer [2001, Chapter 1].) Thus, of the four models produced by choosing from the product {certainty, uncertainty} × {Opportunist, Partisan}, only one engenders parties that, in equilibrium, play different policies: the partisan model with uncertainty. This suggests, if we believe that in reality parties do play different policies, that both uncertainty and partisanship are important features of reality.

D. MULTI-DIMENSIONAL POLITICAL COMPETITION

Unfortunately, both the Hotelling-Downs and the Wittman-Nash models have a severe limitation: they only reliably produce equilibria when the policy space, T, is unidimensional, that is, can be represented as a subset of the real line. Thus, in the application of tax policy, we can only model one-parameter families of tax policies. This is a severe limitation because much – or perhaps virtually all – of political competition involves trade-offs between policies in different arenas. Parties typically present platforms that announce policies on many issues, and they tailor those platforms to assemble support from voters who have a variety of preferences on the issue space.

The relevant theorem states that interior Hotelling-Downs equilibrium generically fails to exist if the dimension of the policy space is

---

[8] I have presented another model that endogenizes parties that care about expected welfare of constituents, but does not require adding up the utility functions of party members: the Condorcet-Nash (CN) model. It is described in Roemer [2001, section 5.3]. In the CN model, each party chooses a member to represent the party as its candidate, and that member plays with his or her own policy preferences. The idea is reminiscent of, but not the same as, the citizen-candidate models of Osborne and Slivinski (1996) and Besley and Coate (1997). However, existence in the CN model fails with multi-dimensional policy spaces.

greater than one.[9] If the policy space is compact, there are sometimes equilibria on the boundary, but they continue to have the property that both parties, unrealistically, propose the same platform. The situation with Wittman-Nash equilibrium is somewhat better. In some models with multi-dimensional policy spaces, Wittman-Nash equilibrium exists generically, and in some models it is generically non-existent. There is no simple characterization of when each of those situations occurs, but they both occur. (For details, see Roemer [2001, Chapter 8].) One cannot depend on the Wittman model either to capture multi-dimensional political competition.

The reaction of political scientists to the generic non-existence of Hotelling-Downs equilibrium has been, in large part, to believe that *policy cycling should be observed in the real world.* A policy cycle occurs when each party proposes a best response to the latest proposal of the other party, and this sequence continues forever because there is no pair of policies whose members are mutual best responses to each other. There are many papers in the literature that look for policy cycling in actual political situations. (For a discussion of the cycling literature, see Hinich and Munger [1997].) That this research strategy was followed shows the power of a formal model: the main model of political equilibrium possesses no equilibrium, therefore researchers concluded there was no equilibrium in real-world politics.

The alternative conclusion would be, of course, that the Hotelling-Downs model is not the right model of political competition. Faced with the observation that we do see (something that looks like an) equilibrium in party competition, one should probably discard the Hotelling-Downs model, at least in the ubiquitous case of multi-issue politics.

In the remainder of this chapter, I present a model that seems to produce reliably equilibria with multi-dimensional political competition.[10] The model introduces the idea that the decision makers in parties are not monolithic, but have different interests. We say that party activists

---

[9] Roemer [2001], Theorems 6.1 and 6.2.

[10] For a more thorough and rigorous development of the PUNE concept, see Roemer [2001, Chapters 8 and 13].

divide into *factions*. In particular, there is a faction that is concerned
solely with winning office, whom we call the Opportunists, and a faction concerned with maximizing the expected welfare of constituents,
whom we call the Reformists. We propose that there is a third faction as
well that is concerned with publicity of the party's views, which we call
the Militants. I do not wish to identify faction members with citizens
of particular types. Think of party activists as professional politicians,
who comprise a small subset (measure zero) of the citizenry, and are
motivated by professional or ideological concerns.

I state the goals of these factions formally. Suppose the partition of
voter types into the constituencies of the two parties is $H = A \cup B$. We
define, as earlier, the utility functions V^A and V^B as the average of the
utility functions of the two constituencies. Then the payoff functions
of the three factions in party A are:

$$P_{\text{Opp}}^A(t^1, t^2) = \pi(t^1, t^2),$$
$$P_{\text{Ref}}^A(t^1, t^2) = \pi(t^1, t^2)V^A(t^1) + (1 - \pi(t^1, t^2))V^A(t^2),$$
$$P_{\text{Mil}}^A(t^1, t^2) = V^A(t^1).$$

Thus, the Opportunists are the *dramatis personae* in the Hotelling-
Downs model, the Reformists are those of the Wittman model, and the
Militants are new: they want to propose a policy as close as possible to
the ideal policy of the party's constituents.

In like manner, party B has the analogous three factions.

It is convenient, at this point, to adopt a new convention as to how
voters who are indifferent between the policies of the two parties vote.
We stipulate that, in a model with parties, if h is indifferent between
two policies, he or she votes for the policy of the party of which he or
she is a member. Because, in what follows, every individual is a member
of a party, this specifies how all indifferent types vote (always, modulo,
the aggregate uncertainty that we have discussed).

We now define a *party-unanimity Nash equilibrium* (PUNE) as:

(1) a partition of types into two parties, $H = A \cup B$, $A \cap B = \emptyset$;
(2) a pair of policies (t^A, t^B) such that:
    (a) Given t^B, there is no policy $t \in T$ such that:

for all $J = Opp, Ref, Mil$ $P_J^A(t, t^B) \geq P_J^A(t^A, t^B)$, with at least one strict inequality;

(b) Given t^A there is no policy $t \in T$ such that:

for all $J=Opp, Ref, Mil$ $P_J^B(t^A, t) \geq P_J^B(t^A, t^B)$, with at least one strict inequality;

(3) for all $h \in A$, $v(t^A, h) \geq v(t^B, h)$ and for all $h \in B$, $v(t^B, h) \geq v(t^A, h)$.

Condition (2a) says that facing the opposition's proposal t^B, there is no policy in T that can improve the payoffs of all three factions in party A. Condition (2b) makes the analogous statement for the factions of party B. In other words, given t^B, policy t^A is *Pareto efficient* for the three factions in party A, and given t^A, policy t^B is Pareto efficient for the three factions of B.

Thus, we can view policy t^A as the outcome of efficient bargaining among A's factions, when facing t^B, and t^B as the outcome of efficient bargaining among B's factions, when facing t^A. A PUNE is a pair of policies, each of which is a *bargaining solution* among the factions of a party, when facing the policy proposed by the other. All we use here is the characterization of efficient bargaining as a policy that is Pareto efficient for the set of bargainers.

Condition (3) states that party membership is stable in the sense that every party member prefers his or her party's policy to the opposition's policy. We can also think of (3) as modeling good representation. The Militants and Reformists in party J form the utility function V^J to be the average utility of those who support them; this is assured by (3). Thus, the coalition of those who vote for a party and the coalition whom the party represents are identical. This condition was used in Baron (1993) in the context of endogenous party formation, and was treated more generally in Caplin and Nalebuff (1997).

What are the relative powers of the three factions in the internal bargaining in a party? We say nothing about that, and therefore we can expect that, if there are any PUNEs, there will be many of them, corresponding to different relative bargaining strengths.

It is not difficult to show that the Reformists are gratuitous in this formulation: *exactly the same set of equilibria* will exist if there were only Opportunists and Militants within parties. (In a sense, the Reformists are a convex combination of the Opportunists and Militants.) Thus, for the purposes of equilibrium analysis, we can eliminate the Reformists. This means that there is *one* number that specifies the relative bargaining power of the Opportunists in party A relative to the Militants, and one number that specifies the relative bargaining power of the Opportunists in B relative to its Militants – thus, two free parameters in the model. It is therefore not surprising that there is, generically, a two-dimensional manifold of PUNEs, if there are any.

Indeed, the important fact is that, even with large dimensional policy spaces, PUNEs often (if not always) exist. I have no general proof of the existence of a two-manifold of PUNEs, but in a variety of applications with finite dimensional policy spaces that I have studied, I have not failed to find such a manifold of PUNEs. Thus, conceptualizing parties as comprised of factions solves – often, at least – the problem of equilibrium existence in multi-dimensional politics.

Indeed, we can say something more about the nature of inter-faction bargaining. With sufficient convexity, we can view the bargaining as Nash bargaining. Let (A, B, t^A, t^B) be a PUNE. Suppose that the functions $\log \pi(\cdot, t^B)$ and $\log(V^A(\cdot) - V^A(t^B))$ are concave. Because there is no policy in T that can make both of these functions larger than they are at t^A – that follows from the fact that (t^A, t^B) is a PUNE – the point $(\log \pi(t^A, t^B), \log(V^A(t^A) - V^A(t^B)))$ must be on the boundary of the convex set:

$$R = \{(x, y) \mid x = \log \pi(t, t^B), y$$
$$= \log(V^A(t) - V^A(t^B)), \quad \text{for some} \quad t \in T, V^A(t) \geq V^A(t^B)\}$$

illustrated in Figure 2.2. We have drawn the line of slope $-\gamma$ that is tangent to R at that point.

Now consider the following bargaining game between the Opportunists and Militants in party A. The Opportunists wish to maximize $\pi(t, t^B)$, over T. Should the bargaining break down, party B wins the election by default, and so the impasse utility for A's Opportunists is zero probability of victory. The Militants in A wish to maximize $V^A(t)$. Should the bargaining break down, the only policy that voters see is t^B,

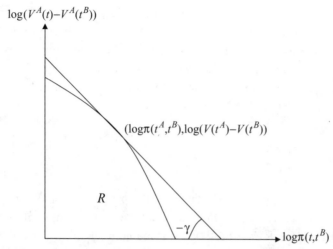

Figure 2.2. PUNE as a generalized Nash bargaining solution.

and so the impasse utility for the Militants is $V^A(t^B)$. Suppose the bargaining strength of the Opportunists relative to the Militants is γ. The Nash product, whose maximum is the solution of this Nash bargaining game, is:

$$(\pi(t, t^B) - 0)^{\gamma}(V^A(t) - V^A(t^B)).$$

Maximizing this Nash product is equivalent to maximizing its logarithm:

$$\gamma \log \pi(t, t^B) + \log(V^A(t) - V^A(t^B)).$$

But Figure 2.2 shows us that this function is maximized precisely at the policy t^A. We have therefore shown that t^A is the outcome of Nash bargaining between A's Opportunists and Militants, when facing t^B. An analogous statement holds for party B, as long as the analogous log-concavity assumption is satisfied. Therefore, with sufficient convexity, every PUNE can be viewed as comprised of two *Nash bargaining solutions*, one each between the factions of each party.

Conversely, it is easy to see that any pair of Nash bargaining solutions that are best responses to each other comprise a PUNE.

I now present a second story that gives rise to exactly the same equilibrium concept. The activists in each party, in this scenario, comprise two factions, the Opportunists and the Guardians. The Opportunists are as before; the Guardians wish to defend the interests of the party's constituents, in the sense of assuring that the Opportunists do not propose a policy that is *unsatisfactory* for the constituents. Thus, within party A, the bargaining between the two factions can be modeled as:

$$\max_t \pi(t, t^B)$$

subject to

$$V^A(t) \geq k^A;$$

that is, the Opportunists maximize the probability of victory, subject to an insistence by the Guardians that the average utility of the party's constituency does not fall below some number k^A. Clearly, the larger k^A, the tougher the Guardians are. A similar program characterizes bargaining in party B. An equilibrium is a policy pair (t^A, t^B), each of which solves the appropriate party's program for a given pair of numbers (k^A, k^B), and satisfies condition (3) of the definition of PUNE. We again will have a two-dimensional manifold of equilibria, parameterized by the pairs (k^A, k^B).

It is not difficult to see that these equilibria are exactly the equilibria of the story with Opportunists, Militants, and Reformists.

Thus, PUNE captures the idea that there are different forces within parties that bargain with each other – forces that desire only to win office, and forces that desire to do well by the party's constituents or members. One finds reference to such forces in many party histories. For instance, Carl Schorske (1955), in his classic history of the German Social Democratic Party, discusses the party bureaucrats, the trade-union leadership, and the radicals. The bureaucrats pursued party power, the trade-union leadership were reformists who were concerned with the welfare of workers but not with party power, and the radicals, such as Rosa Luxemburg and Karl Kautsky, used the party primarily as a vehicle for publicizing what they considered to be the ideal policy of the working class. The radicals were not particularly concerned with winning elections, at least in the short run.

One finds many references to opportunists and militants or guardians in history, but almost no references to reformists, that is, politicians who were concerned with maximizing the *expected utility* of constituents.

This is not too surprising: expected utility is a subtle (and relatively recent) concept. It is therefore gratifying that the Reformists in our model are gratuitous: whether or not they exist, the set of equilibria is the same. The existence of Reformists will only alter *which* equilibrium is selected – that is, the relative bargaining strengths of the factions – assuming that we wish to discuss equilibrium selection.

In fact, more generally, there might be many factions in a party, each of which wishes to maximize a payoff function of the form

$$(\pi(t, t^B))^{\alpha_i}(V^A(t) - V^A(t^B))^{1-\alpha_i},$$

for some $\alpha_i \in [0, 1]$. In particular, for the Opportunists, $\alpha_i = 1$; for the Militants, $\alpha_i = 0$; and for the Reformists, we will soon observe that $\alpha_i = \frac{1}{2}$. But even if factions have many different values of α_i, the upshot is that the model is equivalent to one with only Militants and Opportunists, as long as both the Militants and Opportunists are among the existing factions. (By 'equivalent,' I mean 'possesses the same equilibrium set.')

Why do we not specify the relative bargaining strengths of the factions as data of the model, and hence derive unique, or locally unique, equilibria? The answer is that we cannot be sure that equilibrium will exist, with respect to any given pre-specified pair of relative bargaining strengths.

Consider Figure 2.3, which represents schematically the two-manifold of equilibria, in the space of pairs of relative bargaining strengths of the Opportunists in the two parties. Each axis of the figure measures the relative bargaining strength of the Opportunists (with respect to the Militants) in one of the parties. In my experience, for any particular model, we can be confident that the set G is non-empty and indeed has a non-empty interior, but we cannot say much, in the general case, about G, and hence whether it will contain any pre-specified point.

We can observe that the point $(1,1)$ in this space corresponds to the Wittman-Nash equilibrium. To see this, note that, if $(1,1)$ is in G, then there will be a PUNE (t^A, t^B), where

$$t^A = \arg\max_t \pi(t, t^B)(V^A(t) - V^A(t^B)) \text{ and}$$
$$t^B = \arg\max_t (1 - \pi(t^A, t))(V^B(t) - V^B(t^A)),$$

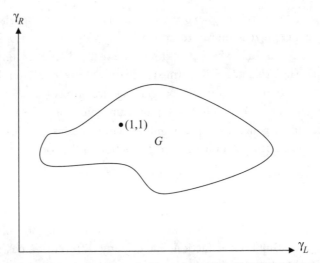

Figure 2.3. A parameterization of the PUNE manifold in the space of relative bargaining powers.

where we have set the relative bargaining strength of the Opportunists to unity. But we can write:

$$\pi(t, t^B)(V^A(t) - V^A(t^B))$$
$$= \pi(t, t^B)V^A(t) + (1 - \pi(t, t^B))V^A(t^B) - V^A(t^B)$$
$$= P^A_{\text{Ref}}(t, t^B) - V^A(t^B) \cong P^A_{\text{Ref}}(t, t^B)$$

where, in the last term, we have dropped a gratuitous constant, and so t^A is also the maximum of the Reformists' payoff function in A, when facing t^B. In like manner, the second equation here is equivalent to the maximization of the Reformists' payoff function in party B. Consequently, a PUNE in which the relative bargaining strengths of the Opportunists in both parties are equal is indeed a simple Wittman-Nash equilibrium.

This allows us to understand, to some degree, the existence question for Wittman-Nash equilibrium in multi-dimensional policy spaces. For a given model, either $(1,1)$ is in the interior of the set G, or it is not. In the former case, Wittman-Nash equilibrium is generic for the model – that is, a small perturbation of the parameters of the model will perturb the equilibrium manifold G slightly, and $(1,1)$ will stay in the manifold. If

(1,1) is not in G, or is not in its interior, then Wittman-Nash equilibrium is generically non-existent for that model.

In other words, PUNE is a generalization of Wittman-Nash equilibrium. Any Wittman-Nash equilibrium is a PUNE. But Wittman-Nash equilibrium often fails to exist, while PUNE often does exist.

Indeed, it is not difficult to see that a Hotelling-Downs equilibrium, if it exists, is also a PUNE. Thus PUNE is an extension to the multi-dimensional policy space environment of both the classical concepts I have described in this chapter. A precise statement is the following:

Definition: A Hotelling-Downs equilibrium (t^1, t^2) is *strict* if for every policy $s \neq t^2$, $\pi(t^1, s) > \frac{1}{2}$, and for every $s \neq t^1$, $\pi(s, t^2) < \frac{1}{2}$. A Wittman-Nash equilibrium (t^1, t^2) is *regular* if $0 < \pi(t^1, t^2) < 1$ and $V^1(t^1) > V^1(t^2)$ and $V^2(t^2) > V^2(t^1)$, where $\{V^1, V^2\}$ are the parties' VNM utility functions.

Theorem 2.1. *Every regular Wittman-Nash equilibrium is a PUNE. Every strict Hotelling-Downs equilibrium is a PUNE.*

Proof: See Roemer (2001), Theorem 8.1, p. 150. ∎

Let me try to indicate why PUNEs typically exist in the multi-dimensional context, while Hotelling-Downs equilibria and Wittman-Nash equilibria do not. A payoff function on $T \times T$ is, from the set-theoretic viewpoint, a complete binary relation on $T \times T$ because it represents an order on $T \times T$. Saying that the Opportunists and Militants must agree to deviate from one policy to another is formally equivalent to saying that the *party*'s payoff binary relation is the *intersection* of the pay-off binary relations of the two factions. This is a quasi-order[11] on $T \times T$. Thus, PUNEs are Nash equilibria of a game played between two quasi-orders.

Now, Nash equilibrium in the Hotelling-Downs game, on a multi-dimensional policy space, fails to exist because, definitionally, one player can always find a deviation that makes him or her better off.

---

[11] A quasi-order is a reflexive, transitive binary relation that is not necessarily complete.

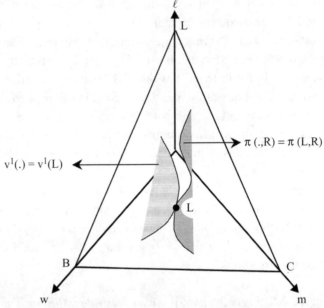

Figure 2.4. Osculating faction indifference curves in a PUNE allocation.

However, if *two* payoff functions have to be satisfied to implement a deviation from a given point, this is much harder to accomplish. Evidently, the objectives of the Opportunists and Militants are sufficiently orthogonal that there are many pairs of policies that are deviation-proof. It is harder to deviate if the payoff binary relation is incomplete than if it is complete, for many possible moves are immediately disqualified because an incomplete binary relation *cannot make a judgment* about them.

I next describe how one computes PUNEs in the case of a finite dimensional policy space. Let T be the plane, for purposes of illustration. Let (A, B, t^A, t^B) be a PUNE for the model $\langle H, \mathbf{F}, T, v, \beta \rangle$: note the abstract specification of the political environment is exactly as in the unidimensional case, except now T is not unidimensional. We define the function $\varphi(t^1, t^2, h) = v(t^1, h) - v(t^2, h)$.

Now consider the space T, where, in Figure 2.4, I have drawn the indifference curves of the Opportunists and Militants, or Guardians, in A, at the point t^A. In the example the figure is taken from, the policy space is the two-simplex of vectors (w, m, ℓ) whose components sum to a constant. If the equilibrium is interior in the policy space, as illustrated, then these indifference curves must be tangent at that point – there is no possibility of mutual welfare increases for both the Opportunists and the Militants. Therefore, the gradients of the payoff functions of the two factions must point in opposite directions. Consequently, necessary conditions for an interior PUNE are as follows:

$$A = \{h \in H \mid \varphi(t^A, t^B, h) > 0\}$$
$$B = \{h \in H \mid \varphi(t^A, t^B, h) \leq 0\}$$
$$V^A(t) = \int_{h \in A} v(t, h) d\mathbf{F}(h)$$
$$V^B(t) = \int_{h \in B} v(t, h) d\mathbf{F}(h)$$
$$\nabla V^A(t) = -x_A \nabla_A \pi (t^A, t^B), \text{ some } x_A \geq 0$$
$$\nabla V^B(t) = -x_B \nabla_B (1 - \pi(t^A, t^B)), \text{ some } x_B \geq 0$$

If the dimension of the policy space is n, then the last two vector equations comprise $2n$ equations in $2n + 2$ unknowns (the policy variables plus the two Lagrangian multipliers). Thus, if there is one solution, there will, generically, be a two-manifold of solutions, if the premises of the implicit function theorem hold.

PUNEs that lie on the boundary of the policy space, which often occur in economic applications, can similarly be characterized as the solution of $2n$ equations in $2n + 2$ unknowns, by use of the Kuhn-Tucker theorem, or Farkas' Lemma. Finding solutions to these equations, in particular applications, is feasible by computer. Indeed, one often can pave out the equilibrium manifold using randomization methods.

One interesting characteristic of the equilibrium manifold – again, there is no theorem – is that it is often quite locally concentrated in the policy space. So, although we do not pre-specify the relative bargaining strengths of the factions, the set of possible equilibria often is not large. In other words, we often do not lose much precision by remaining agnostic about the details of the internal party bargaining process.

E. RECAPITULATION

Let me conclude this chapter with a brief recapitulation. The first successful formal model of political competition was that of Harold Hotelling and later Anthony Downs, which, however, presented an unrealistic view of politics, one in which competition was completely dominated by opportunist political entrepreneurs. Given the high stakes of state control, it is hard to imagine that such a model could describe a reality where there are groups with sharply variant interests within the polity. It is indeed interesting to note that, in economic theory, the agency problem did not appear in formal models until the 1970s, while in political theory, the first formal models exaggerated in an extreme form the problem of agency. The Wittman model, proposed some fifteen years after Downs wrote, went to the other extreme, representing political parties as maximizers of partisan preferences with no office-holding interests.

In addition to their having rather one-sided views of political competition, neither of these models performs well, in the sense of possessing equilibria, except when policy spaces are unidimensional; because multi-dimensional political competition is ubiquitous in reality, something else is needed. There was a period in political science in which the non-existence of Hotelling-Downs equilibrium with multi-dimensional policy spaces led researchers to look for cycling, in real politics. The equilibrium theorist, however, will look for a conception of equilibrium that works in those contexts.

We have proposed a model of politics in which parties are complex institutions: bargaining occurs between groups of political entrepreneurs, some of whom are Downsian in character and some of whom are interested in representing constituents. This model appears to solve the equilibrium existence problem with multi-dimensional policy spaces, at least in many instances, and because party histories are replete with descriptions of intra-party conflict over strategy, we have some hope that the model represents reality more faithfully than either the Hotelling-Downs or Wittman-Nash concepts, both of which it extends.

CHAPTER 3

Democratic Competition over
Educational Investment

A. THE POLITICO-ECONOMIC ENVIRONMENT

We will model a society that reproduces itself over many generations. At the initial date, there are households led by adults (parents) who are characterized by a distribution of human capital, that is, capacities to produce income. (As I wrote earlier, human capital has other values for a person.) Each parent has one child. The human capital the child will have, when he or she becomes an adult, is a monotone increasing function of his or her parent's level of human capital and the amount that is invested in his or her education. This relationship is deterministic, and describes the educational production function for all children. Thus, more investment is needed to bring a child from a poor (low human capital) family up to a given level of human capital than a child from a wealthier family. All parents have the same utility function: a parent cares about his or her household's consumption (which will be his or her after-tax income), and the human capital his or her child will come to have as an adult. We will, for simplicity, assume that adults do not value leisure. Thus, income will be earned inelastically with respect to taxation.

Initially, let us assume that educational finance is purely public, an assumption we will later relax. The polity of adults, at each date, must make four political decisions: how much to tax themselves, how to partition the tax revenues between a redistributive budget for households' current consumption and the educational (investment) budget, how to allocate the budget for redistribution among adults, and how to target the educational budget as investment in particular children, according to their type (that is, their parents' level of human capital). Once these political decisions are implemented, a distribution of human capital is determined for the next generation. When the present children become adults, characterized by that distribution of human capital, they face the same four political decisions. We wish to study the asymptotic distribution of human capital of this dynamic process.

In the society we have described, a child is characterized by the family into which he or she is born because his or her capacity to transform educational investment into future earning power is determined by his or her family background and the proxy is his or her parents' human capital. We imagine that the transmission of 'culture' to the child is indicated by the parents' human capital endowment. The child's capacity to successfully absorb educational investment, and transform it into human capital, is a circumstance beyond his or her control, and so a society of this kind that wishes to *equalize opportunities* for all children would compensate children from poorer families with more educational investment. Equality of opportunity would be achieved when all adults come to have the same human capital, because, as children in the previous generation, the compensation for disadvantageous circumstances is complete. In the real world, equality of opportunity does not require equalizing outcomes in this way because people remain responsible for some aspect of their condition (the effort they expend, for example), even after the necessary compensation for disadvantage has been made. But in our model, there is no such element of personal responsibility, and so, if we take equality of opportunity as our conception of justice, then justice will have been achieved exactly when the wage-earning capacities of all adults are equal.

We will stipulate a democratic process for solving society's political problems at each generation, and our focus will be on that democratic process. We employ the PUNE concept of democratic political equilibrium, which takes as data the distribution of preferences of the polity over a given policy space, and produces as output an endogenous partition of the polity into two political parties, a policy proposal by each party, and a probability that each party will win the election. We suppose that an election occurs, and the policy of the victorious party is implemented. Our procedure begins with a distribution of adult human capital at date 0, which will determine the distribution of adult preferences at date 0, and thus initialize this stochastic dynamic process.

Although I have described the political choice as consisting of four independent decisions, we will in fact model the political problem as one on an infinite dimensional policy space. That policy space, denoted as T, will consist of pairs of functions (ψ, r) where $\psi(h)$ is the after-tax household income of an adult with human capital h, and $r(h)$ is the public educational investment in a child from a family where the parent has human capital h. These functions will be restricted only to be continuous, to jointly satisfy a budget constraint, and to satisfy an upper and lower bound on their derivatives, when the derivatives exist.

The present analysis therefore marks a technical advance over analyses in political economy that rely on equilibrium concepts that are non-vacuous only when policy spaces are unidimensional. The advance, I believe, is not merely technical. It is surely artificial to restrict a democratic polity's choice of policies to ones with simple mathematical properties, such as linearity. Characterizing the political equilibrium with no such restrictions means that we are able to model the democratic struggle as *ruthlessly competitive*: no holds, in the sense of unmotivated restrictions on the nature of policy proposals, are barred. A quick glance at history will show that tax policy is extremely complex in democracies: almost all democracies possess statutory piece-wise linear income taxation (although Germany had a system with continuously increasing marginal tax rates). It turns out that, in our model, equilibrium tax policies are piece-wise linear with a small number of pieces, although the policy space permits much more general forms.

Indeed, we will show in Chapter 4 that the infinite-dimensional analysis gives qualitatively different results from a unidimensional Downsian analysis of the same problem. If one thinks, as I do, that political parties in reality choose policies from a policy space of large dimension, then the extra work required to model that choice will not be for naught.

Many authors, over the past decade, have studied the relationship between education and equality in democracies.[1] Some of the work models the problem in an overlapping generations framework, and some of the work endogenizes the political decision concerning the funding of public education. In all the work of which I am aware in which policy is endogenized, the policy space is unidimensional; taxes are proportional income or wealth taxes. Public educational investment is always distributed equally to all students; what variation there is in the amount of education an individual receives is either due to the existence of private supplements or to variations in time spent in school across wealth levels, where that choice is made by the individual. In almost all these publications, public education has an equalizing effect on incomes, at least in the long run. (That effect may not hold true at all times because children from richer families may be able to spend more time in school than children from poorer families.) This is not surprising, if the same amount is invested in all children. Generally, more inequality in the initial distribution of income/human capital leads to higher taxation, more public education, and hence more growth.

The general characteristic that distinguishes the work alluded to from my study is that its authors postulate more heterogeneity among citizens than I do. In the publications mentioned, citizens differ not only in their levels of human capital and/or income, but sometimes in their preferences, often in their (randomly realized) talents, and sometimes in the neighborhoods in which they live. Sometimes the democracy is incomplete, and citizens differ in their voting rights. On the other hand, the political model is typically extremely simple: majority vote over a proportional tax rate. The present study complements this work: it abstracts from heterogeneity in the composition of the citizenry, with the sole exception of the differentiation in human-capital endowments, and articulates to a much greater degree the political mechanism. In particular, it is a general characteristic of policies of educational finance, in my model, that students from richer families

---

[1] See, among others, Glomm and Ravikumar (1992), Saint-Paul and Verdier (1993), Zhang (1996), Durlauf (1996), Gradstein and Justman (1996), Bénabou (1996), Turrini (1998), Fernandez and Rogerson (1998), Cardak (1999), Bourguignon and Verdier (2000), and Glomm and Ravikumar (2003).

receive more public investment in their education, a feature that is at least true of American democracy, among the advanced countries, and appears ubiquitous in democracies at low levels of economic development. It is, moreover, a feature of all democracies, to the extent that it is the case that those who acquire tertiary education are primarily from more well-to-do families. In the dynamic models of the existing literature, this does not occur. To be sure, there is a literature in which educational investment is financed by local property taxes, in which richer towns fund schools at a higher level than poorer ones (see, for example, Epple and Romer [1991]). With the exception of Bénabou (1996) and Fernandez and Rogerson (1998), however, these models are not dynamic. Fernandez and Rogerson study an OLG model that stipulates the existence of two towns, and citizens sort themselves into what become a rich and a poor town, resulting in high and low levels of educational finance, due to local funding of schools. State funding equalizes educational investment, with a consequent equalizing effect on income. In our study, however, due to the large policy space, funding at the state (i.e., national) level will, in general, continue to favor investment in the children of rich families, and so the extent to which education will equalize, over the long run, levels of human capital is unclear.

B. PREFERENCES

We begin by stating the preferences of the adults, who are the political actors. A parent's utility function is

$$u(x, h') = \log x + \gamma \log h'$$

where x is the family's consumption and h' is the human capital the child will (come to) have as an adult. We measure the child's human capital by his or her earning power, and a person with human capital h earns h in a unit of time. Earlier I wrote that adults derive welfare directly from their human capital, and so one might wish to add a term to the utility function showing that the parent cares about his or her own human capital, as well as his or her income. But that term would be a constant at the time the parent is a decision maker and the adult's human capital is unchangeable, so it would be gratuitous to include it in the utility function.

We furthermore assume, as in Chapter 2, that these utility functions are von Neumann-Morgenstern, and are unit comparable, and so it makes sense to add them up.

C. TECHNOLOGY

The educational technology is

$$h' = \alpha h^b r^c$$

where h is the parent's human capital, h' is human capital the child will come to have as an adult, and r is investment in the child's education. We think of the input of parental human capital as operating through household culture, and perhaps social and professional connections of the parent as well. (High-wage parents can find high-wage jobs for their children.) For reasons explained in Chapter 1, I assume that all children possess the same degree of talent.

Depending on whether $b + c$ is less than, equal to, or greater than one, we say the returns to scale in education are decreasing, constant, or increasing, respectively.

With this educational technology, returns to education are purely private: my child's wage depends only on what is invested in my child. In Chapter 5, we will modify the production function to include an endogenous-growth element, modeling the idea that there are positive externalities in education so that educational investment has a public-good aspect.

D. THE POLICY SPACE

Political parties will choose, as their platform, a pair of functions

$$\psi : H \to \mathbf{R}_+, \quad r : H \to \mathbf{R}_+,$$

where $\psi(h)$ is the after-tax income that an h family will receive, and $r(h)$ is the public educational investment in children from h families. Let the distribution of parental human capital, which is the same as pre-tax income, at a given date be given by a probability measure $\mathbf{F}$ on the non-negative real numbers with mean μ. We assume that the support of $\mathbf{F}$ is the non-negative real line, and that $\mathbf{F}$ is equivalent to the Lebesgue measure, although these assumptions could be dispensed with.[2] Then feasibility requires:

$$\int (\psi(h) + r(h)) d\mathbf{F}(h) = \mu. \tag{3.1}$$

We insist as well that ψ and r be continuous functions. Denote the *total resource bundle* going to an h family by

$$X(h) = \psi(h) + r(h);$$

we restrict policies by requiring that the derivative of X, when it exists, be bounded above and below[3]:

$$\psi'(h) + r'(h) \leq 1 \tag{3.2}$$
$$\psi'(h) + r'(h) \geq 0 \tag{3.3}$$

Inequality (3.2) says that there cannot be intervals where there is redistribution from the relatively poor to the relatively rich, in the sense that the total resource bundle increases faster than pre-tax income. Inequality (3.3) says the redistribution from the relatively rich to the relatively poor cannot be excessive, in the sense that the total resource bundle decreases with pre-tax income.

Consider the *laissez-faire* policy, in which there is no taxation, and parents are assumed to finance education from private income. In that case, $X(h) = h$, and so $X'(h) = 1$. Thus, (3.2) says that the tax regime cannot be more regressive than laissez-faire. In particular, laissez-faire is feasible.

[2] Two measures are equivalent if their null sets are the same.

[3] To be mathematically precise, we need only require that the function X be non-decreasing and satisfy the Lipschitz condition $X(h^2) - X(h^1) \leq h^2 - h^1$ for all $h^2 > h^1$.

Thus, our policy space is

$$T = \{(\psi, r) \mid (\psi, r) \text{ continuous and (3.1), (3.2), and (3.3) hold}\}.$$

Further comment on the constraints that characterize T is warranted. The present analysis (like all analyses) makes some assumptions that are not formally modeled. One is that policies must be continuous. Another is that the derivatives on X must lie in the interval $[0,1]$. I think that these assumptions are justified by the norms of advanced democracy: those norms put restrictions on what kinds of policy it is ethically acceptable for a political party to propose. Continuity is such a restriction: it is, if you will, an extension of the norm of non-arbitrariness. (If a policy is discontinuous, then types that are almost identical are treated very differently.) Similarly, one observes, in an advanced democracy, there is no fiscal policy that *is seen* to violate the condition on the derivatives of X.[4] To tax at a marginal rate of greater than one would be viewed as unfair to the talented, as well as seriously deleterious to incentives, and to tax at a rate of less than zero would be viewed as expropriation of the untalented.

It would be intellectually preferable to derive the continuity of policies, and the bounds on the derivatives of the total resource bundle, from the politics of competition rather than imposing them as constraints. I do not see how to do this in a simple way, and am content to impose these conditions as definitional of the policy space. One might wish to call these inequalities social or political norms, as they are imposed constraints on policy, which are motivated by the view that such norms do indeed constrain policy.

The analogue of assumptions (3.2) and (3.3) in the standard model of unidimensional affine taxation is that the (constant) marginal tax rate lies between zero and one. This assumption is traditional, although it must – there too – be considered a social norm in the sense of being an underived restriction on the policy space.

As I said, the policy space T is infinite dimensional. It contains very complicated functions. We will see that the piece-wise linear functions

---

[4] It is a more delicate question to ask whether, after the incidence of taxation and benefits are accounted for, this condition is violated.

play a special role: indeed, equilibrium policies will always be piece-wise linear.

We can now write the indirect utility function of an adult on policies:

$$
\begin{aligned}
v(\psi, r, h) &= \log \psi(h) + \gamma \log \alpha h^b r(h)^c \\
&= \log \psi(h) + \gamma (\log \alpha h^b) + \gamma c \log r(h) \qquad (3.4) \\
&\cong \log \psi(h) + \gamma c \log r(h)
\end{aligned}
$$

where, in the last line, I drop a term that is gratuitous because the decision maker's human capital h is fixed. Thus, parental utility is a Cobb-Douglas function of after-tax income and educational investment in his or her child.

A standard move, in models of this kind, is to impose an incentive compatibility condition that says that an adult with human capital h should not be able to increase his or her welfare by working at a lower wage rate. The local version of this condition, from (3.4), is:

$$
\frac{\psi'(h)}{\psi(h)} + \gamma c \frac{r'(h)}{r(h)} \geq 0. \qquad (3.5)
$$

We do not impose (3.5) as a restriction on the policy space because doing so would render the analysis below extremely difficult. It would convert what will be concave optimization problems on an infinite-dimensional space into non-concave problems that the present author cannot solve. Nevertheless, the equilibrium policies in our analysis will satisfy (3.5).

E. POLITICAL EQUILIBRIUM CONCEPTS

A PUNE for this model, given the distribution **F**, consists of:

(P1) a partition $L \cup R = \mathbf{R}_+$, $L = [0, h^*)$, $R = [h^*, \infty)$
(P2) party utility functions

$$
V^L(\psi, r) = \int_0^{h^*} (\log \psi(h) + \gamma c \log r(h)) d\mathbf{F}(h),
$$

$$V^R(\psi, r) = \int_{h^*}^{\infty} (\log \psi(h) + \gamma c \log r(h)) d\mathbf{F}(h),$$

(P3) a pair of policies $(\psi^L, r^L), (\psi^R, r^R)$ such that:

(a) there is no

$(\psi, r) \in T$, such that $V^L(\psi, r) \geq V^L(\psi^L, r^L)$ and $\pi((\psi, r), (\psi^R, r^R)) \geq \pi((\psi^L, r^L), (\psi^R, r^R))$, with at least one inequality strict, and

(b) there is no

$(\psi, r) \in T$, such that $V^R(\psi, r) \geq V^R(\psi^R, r^R)$ and $\pi((\psi^L, r^L), (\psi, r)) \leq \pi((\psi^L, r^L), (\psi^R, r^R))$, with at least one inequality strict;

(c) $h \in L \Rightarrow v(\psi^L, r^L; h) \geq v(\psi^R, r^R; h),$

$h \in R \Rightarrow v(\psi^L, r^L; h) \leq v(\psi^R, r^R; h).$

We call the two parties *Left* and *Right* because they represent the bottom and top of the human-capital distribution, respectively.[5]

In this definition, I have not included the Reformist factions, whose payoff functions are the expected average utility of their respective parties' members. The set of PUNEs does not change with their inclusion.

Our first observation will allow us to simplify our problem. It is the following:

Proposition 3.1. *In any PUNE,* $r^L(h) = \gamma c \psi^L(h)$ *for almost all* $h \in L$, *and* $r^R(h) = \gamma c \psi^R(h)$ *for almost all* $h \in R$.

Proof: The proof is easy, and follows from the Cobb-Douglas formulation of parental utility and the fact that there are no external effects in the educational technology. Let $(\hat{\psi}, \hat{r})$ be an equilibrium policy of one of the parties, say Left, let $X = \hat{\psi} + \hat{r}$ be the total resource bundle, and

---

[5] Note that I restrict PUNEs to be equilibria in which the two parties are intervals. There are perhaps other equilibria of a more general form.

suppose $\hat{r}$ is not proportional to $\hat{\psi}$ for a subset of L of positive measure, as in the proposition's statement. If a family h receives $X(h)$ as total resource, it would optimally partition this resource into consumption and investment as follows:

$$\psi(h) = \frac{1}{1+\gamma c}X(h), \quad r(h) = \frac{\gamma c}{1+\gamma c}X(h). \tag{3.6}$$

So the policy (ψ, r) will increase the welfare of some members of Left, and decrease no one's welfare, without changing the function X. Therefore, the Left Militants' payoff increases at (ψ, r). Moreover, any type that preferred Left's policy to Right's will *a fortiori* prefer the policy (ψ, r) to Right's, so the probability of Left victory will not fall. Finally, we observe that

$$\psi' + r' = X',$$

and so, because $(\hat{\psi}, \hat{r})$ satisfied the constraints defining T, so does (ψ, r). Thus, (ψ, r) is a feasible policy. This shows that condition P3(a) was false at $(\hat{\psi}, \hat{r})$, and so, contrary to supposition, the original policy was not a PUNE. The proposition follows, by contradiction.   ∎

Moreover, we may without loss of generality assume that, for $J = L, R$

$$r^J(h) = \gamma c \psi^J(h), \quad h \in H,$$

because it costs a party nothing to distribute the total resource in the individually optimal way to its non-members, as well.

We can therefore, henceforth, conduct all arguments in terms of the total resource bundle X, because we know that ψ and r are derived from X according to (3.6), for both parties. Using (3.6), we can rewrite the parties' utility functions, after eliminating gratuitous constants, as:

$$V^L(X) = \int_0^{h^*} \log X(h)d\mathbf{F}(h), \quad V^R(X) = \int_{h^*}^{\infty} \log X(h)d\mathbf{F}(h).$$

Of course, the constraints defining T are immediately written in terms of X.

Thus, we have reduced the problem of studying policies that are pairs of functions on H to the problem of studying singletons of functions on H. (Clearly, this is the purchase of the Cobb-Douglas assumption.) These are the continuous functions X that are non-decreasing, have slopes no larger than unity, and integrate to μ. We denote this policy space by T^*.

It is not surprising that it is very difficult to characterize PUNEs on this large policy space. We will introduce another concept, the so-called quasi-PUNE. Quasi-PUNEs will be relatively easy to characterize, and we will argue that the quasi-PUNE notion is probably a satisfactory concept of equilibrium.

A quasi-PUNE[6] is:

(Q1) a level of human capital h^* and a partition $L = [0, h^*)$, $R = [h^*, \infty)$, of the polity;

(Q2) party utility functions

$$V^L(X) = \int_0^{h^*} \log X(h)d\mathbf{F}(h),$$

$$V^R(X) = \int_{h^*}^{\infty} \log X(h)d\mathbf{F}(h),$$

(Q3) a pair of total resource functions X^L, X^R in T^* such that
   (a) there exists no policy $X \in T^*$ such that $X(h) \geq X^R(h)$ for all $h \leq h^*$ and $V^L(X) \geq V^L(X^L)$ and $\pi(X, X^R) \geq \pi(X^L, X^R)$, with at least one strict inequality among the last two;
   (b) there exists no policy $X \in T^*$ such $X(h) \geq X^L(h)$ for all $h \geq h^*$ and $V^R(X) \geq V^R(X^R)$ and $\pi(X^L, X) \leq \pi(X^L, X^R)$, with at least one strict inequality among the last two;

---

[6] As in the definition of PUNE, I do not represent the interest of the Reformists in (Q3). They may be included without loss of generality. As in the PUNE, Reformists are easily seen to be gratuitous, in the sense that the set of equilibria is identical, with and without their presence.

(c) for all

$$h \in L, v(X^L, h) \geq v(X^R, h)$$
$$h \in R, v(X^R, h) \geq v(X^L, h)$$

The only difference between PUNEs and quasi-PUNEs is that an extra constraint on the solution is required of the quasi-PUNE: this appears in (Q3)(a) and (Q3)(b). Consider, for example, (Q3)(a). A candidate X for a deviation from X^L must satisfy the additional requirement

"that $X(h) \geq X^R(h)$ for all $h \leq h^*$";

this means that a policy X^L is an acceptable response to X^R only if there is no policy *that preserves the loyalty of all L members* and is an improvement of the payoffs for at least one of the Militant and Opportunist factions without hurting either one. A similar statement holds for acceptable Right deviations, in (Q3)(b).

We may justify this additional requirement as follows. In its bargaining with the Opportunists (and the Reformists), the Militants insist not only that the average welfare of the party's members (constituents) not fall, under a proposed policy deviation, but that the party deliver at least as much to *each* of its members as the opposition proposes to do. Thus the Militants are concerned both with the global welfare of their membership (average utility) and with their local welfare (serve every member at least as well as the opposition proposes to do). Thus, we may think of quasi-PUNEs as PUNEs in which the Militants are *even more militant* with regard to protecting the interests of constituents (members).

Proposition 3.1 continues to hold for quasi-PUNEs. It is immediately clear that:

Proposition 3.2. *Every* PUNE *is a quasi*-PUNE.

This follows because quasi-PUNEs put additional restrictions on admissible deviations. If a pair of policies survives the PUNE test for deviation, *a fortiori* it survives the quasi-PUNE test.

Our strategy will be, henceforth, to study quasi-PUNEs. We leave open the difficult question of where, in the set of quasi-PUNEs, the PUNEs are located. All the results we have will apply to PUNEs, except that some of those results may be vacuous, because PUNEs with the particular properties of quasi-PUNEs that we study may not exist. It would be desirable to be able to carry out the analysis of dynamics for PUNEs, but that appears to be a formidable task. We shall attempt to indicate why in section 3F below.

We next provide a complete characterization of non-trivial quasi-PUNEs – to wit, those in which both parties win with positive probability.

Proposition 3.3. *Let* (h^*, X^L, X^R) *be a quasi-PUNE at which both parties win with positive probability. Then there exists a number* $\bar{y}$ *such that*

$$X^L \text{ solves } \max_{X \in T^*} V^L(X)$$

subject to

$$h \leq h^* \Rightarrow X(h) \geq X^R(h) \quad \text{(L1)} \qquad\qquad \text{(Q*3a)}$$

$$X(h^*) \geq \bar{y} \qquad\qquad\qquad \text{(L2)}$$

$$X^R \text{ solves } \max_{X \in T^*} V^R(X)$$

subject to

$$h \geq h^* \Rightarrow X(h) \geq X^L(h) \quad \text{(R1)} \qquad\qquad \text{(Q*3b)}$$

$$X(h^*) \geq \bar{y} \qquad\qquad\qquad \text{(R2)}$$

and constraints (L2) *and* (R2) *bind. Conversely, if there is a number* $\bar{y}$ *such that* X^L *and* X^R *satisfy* (Q*3a) *and* (Q*3b) *and both parties win with positive probability at this pair of policies, then* (h^*, X^L, X^R) *is a quasi-PUNE.*

Proof: From (Q3)(c) it immediately follows that $X^L(h^*) = X^R(h^*)$ and we may take that common value to be the number $\bar{y}$. Now (Q*3a) is simply a way of stating (Q3)(a); conditions (L1) and (L2) guarantee that the set of voters 'expected' to vote for policy X^L is $[0, h^*]$. Because the probability of victory is strictly increasing in the size of the coalition that supports the policy,[7] when the probability is positive, program (Q^*3a) is one that maximizes the payoff of the Militants subject to guaranteeing a lower bound on the payoff of the Opportunists. Hence $(Q3)(a)$ implies $(Q3^*a)$. Likewise, $(Q3)(b)$ implies $(Q3^*b)$. Clearly $(Q3)(c)$ holds.

The converse argument is equally straightforward.   ■

We will proceed by solving even simpler programs than (Q^*3ab), namely:

$$\max_{X \in T^*} \int_0^{h^*} \log X(h) d\mathbf{F}(h)$$

$$s.t. \qquad\qquad\qquad \text{(SL)}$$

$$X(h^*) \geq \overline{y},$$

and

$$\max_{X \in T^*} \int_{h^*}^{\infty} \log X(h) d\mathbf{F}(h)$$

$$s.t.$$

$$X(h^*) \geq \overline{y} \qquad\qquad \text{(SR)}$$

After solving (SL) and (SR) we will note that, if the constraints in (SL) and (SR) bind, then the other constraints (L1) of (Q^*3a) and (R1) of (Q^*3b) hold, and furthermore, that $(Q3)(c)$ holds, and so these solutions of (SL) and (SR) are indeed quasi-PUNEs.

We now note that (SL) and (SR) are concave programs: they involve maximizing a concave functional (the integral of the logarithm) on a convex set of functions. (Just note that if two functions are in T^*, so is their convex combination, and furthermore, the constraints in (SL) and (SR) are convex constraints.) So, in principle, these are solvable programs provided that a solution exists, which follows from the fact that T^* is compact and the maximand continuous with respect to the sup norm metric for real-valued functions. I recall my earlier remark

---

[7] Here, invoke the fact that $\mathbf{F}$ is equivalent to Lebesgue measure, so that any decrease in the size of the coalition decreases the probability of victory.

about incentive compatibility. Had we included (3.5) as a constraint on the policy space, (SL) and (SR) would be non-concave programming problems, on an infinite-dimensional function space, and solving them appears to be very difficult.

At this juncture, we make an important technical observation. (SL) and (SR) are concave optimization problems, and no fixed-point methods need be employed to solve them. The fortuitous aspect of program (SL) is that *it does not refer to the policy* X^R; likewise, program (SR) does not refer to the policy X^L. Thus the *interaction* between policies, which makes solving for Nash equilibrium an intrinsically difficult problem, has *disappeared* with the formulation of the quasi-PUNE concept. We have, replaced the very difficult problem of finding fixed points in an infinite-dimensional space (the problem of finding PUNEs) with solving two optimization problems. It is this 'trick' that makes our project tractable.

We solve (SL) and (SR) in two steps. In step 1, we characterize the set of ordered pairs $(h^*, \overline{y})$ such that, at the solutions to (SL) and (SR), the constraints in those programs are binding, as required. In step 2, we solve the programs for those values of $(h^*, \overline{y})$.

Step 1 is conceptually simple. Fix a type h^*. First we solve the program:

$$\max_{X \in T^*} \int_0^{h^*} \log X(h) d\mathbf{F}(h); \qquad \text{(SL1)}$$

call its solution X^L; note that existence follows from compactness of T^* and uniqueness from strict concavity of the objective function. Define $y^L(h^*) = X^L(h^*)$. Next we solve the program:

$$\max_{X \in T^*} \log X(h^*), \qquad \text{(SL2)}$$

call its solution X^* and define $y^*(h^*) = X^*(h^*)$. Then it follows by concavity that the values of $\overline{y}$ for which (SL) possesses a solution, and the constraint binds, are exactly

$$y^L(h^*) \leq \overline{y} \leq y^*(h^*).$$

In like manner, there is an interval $[y^R(h^*), y^*(h^*)]$ in which $\bar{y}$ must lie for (SR) to possess a solution in which its constraint binds. We find $y^R(h^*)$ by solving the program:

$$\max_{X \in T^*} \int_{h^*}^{\infty} \log X(h) d\mathbf{F}(h); \qquad\qquad \text{(SR1)}$$

then set $y^R(h^*) = X^R(h^*)$, where X^R is the solution to (SR1).

We have:

Proposition 3.4. *For a given h^*, both (SL) and (SR) possess solutions at which the constraints in those programs are binding if and only if:*

$$\max[y^L(h^*), y^R(h^*)] \leq \bar{y} \leq y^*(h^*). \qquad\qquad (3.7)$$

Proof: First note that if $\bar{y} > y^*(h^*)$, then there is no feasible solution X where $X(h^*) = \bar{y}$. And if $\bar{y} < \max[y^L(h^*), y^R(h^*)]$, then the inequality constraint of the solution of at least one of the programs (SL) or (SR) will *not* be binding. (For example, suppose $\bar{y} < y^L(h^*)$. Then the solution of (SL) will be the solution of (SL1), and the constraint in (SL) will not bind.) Therefore at any pair of solutions to (SL) and (SR) at which the constraints bind, (3.7) must hold.

Conversely, let $\bar{y}$ be a number in the interval defined by (3.7). Then we know that the feasible sets for the two programs are non-empty. By the Weierstrass maximum theorem, the programs (SL) and (SR) possess solutions.[8] Furthermore, the constraint

$$X(h^*) \geq \bar{y}$$

---

[8] Establishing this fact requires showing that, with respect to some topology, the set of functions X in T^* satisfying $X(h^*) \geq \bar{y}$ for $(h^*, \bar{y}) \in \Gamma$ is compact in the linear space of continuous functions and that the functional $\Phi(X) = \int_a^b \log X(h) d F(h)$ is continuous. Indeed, we may choose the topology of uniform convergence. Because the functions $X \in T^*$ satisfy a Lipschitz condition, any sequence of functions in T^* is equicontinuous, and Arzela's theorem (Artémiadis [1976, p. 270]) guarantees that a uniformly convergent subsequence exists; hence T^* is compact in the topology of uniform convergence. To verify that is continuous in the topology of uniform convergence, we need only observe that the integral never diverges to negative infinity on the feasible set.

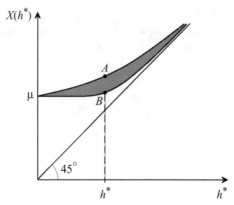

Figure 3.1. The manifold of quasi-PUNEs.

must be binding for both solutions because $\overline{y} \geq \max[y^L(h^*), y^R(h^*)]$, proving the claim.   ∎

In the Appendix, I solve (SL1) , (SL2), and (SR1), and I observe that the interval defined in (3.7) is non-empty for all $h^* > 0$. However, there will be an open interval C in the positive reals of values of h^* for which the probability of victory for both parties at these quasi-PUNEs is positive. (Recall our definition of probability in (2.1). If the random variable that defines electoral uncertainty is uniformly distributed on the interval $[-\beta, \beta]$, then C is the interval $\{h^* | -\beta < \frac{1}{2} - F(h^*) < \beta\}$.) We are, in any case, not interested in quasi-PUNEs where one party has a zero probability of winning: we will assume that the Opportunists have sufficient power to veto these.

In sum, there are quasi-PUNEs for every possible 'pivotal' type $h^* \in C$. Every point in the set

$$\Gamma = \{(h^*, \overline{y}) \,|\, h^* \in C \text{ and } \max[y^L(h^*), y^R(h^*)] \leq \overline{y} \leq y^*(h^*)\} \quad (3.8)$$

characterizes a quasi-PUNE with both parties' winning with positive probability.

Hence Γ is the two-manifold of quasi-PUNEs that interests us. Γ is graphed in Figure 3.1. The points on the lower envelope of Γ are the points where

$$\overline{y} = \max[y^L(h^*), y^R(h^*)];$$

these correspond to equilibria where the Militants in at least one party are as strong as they can possibly be. At all points on this envelope, at least one Militant faction is proposing its ideal policy, the policy in T^* that maximizes the average welfare of its members. For example, if $\bar{y} = y^L(h^*)$, the Left plays the ideal policy of Militants in the quasi-PUNE $(h^*, \bar{y})$. At points on the upper envelope of Γ we have $\bar{y} = y^*(h^*)$. At such points, it immediately follows that *both parties propose the same policy*, the ideal policy of the *pivotal* voter, h^*. These are equilibria where the Opportunists in both parties are as powerful as they can possibly be. Note the apparent similarity to the Hotelling-Downs model, where with opportunist politics, both parties play the *median* ideal policy.

The lower and upper envelopes of Γ then, correspond to equilibria with *ideological* and *opportunist* politics, respectively. These two boundaries play an important role in the following analysis.

The second step of our program involves solving programs (SL) and (SR) for points $(h^*, \bar{y}) \in \Gamma$. The solutions are given in the next proposition.

Proposition 3.5. *Let* $(h^*, \bar{y}) \in \Gamma$. *Then:*

a.   *The solution to* (SL) *is defined by:*

$$
X^L(h) = \begin{cases} \hat{X}_0^L, & 0 \leq h \leq h_L \\ \hat{X}_0^L + (h - h_L), & h_L \leq h \leq h^* \\ \bar{y}, & h > h^* \end{cases}
$$

where $(\hat{X}_0^L, h_L)$ is the simultaneous solution of the two equations:

$$
\hat{X}_0^L + h^* - h_L = \bar{y}, \quad (3.9a)
$$

$$
\hat{X}_0^L + \int_{h_L}^{h^*} (h - h_L)d\mathbf{F}(h) + (1 - F(h^*))(h^* - h_L) = \mu. \quad (3.9b)
$$

We have $\hat{X}_0^L > 0$.

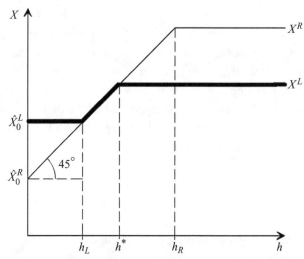

Figure 3.2. Left (bold) and Right policies in a quasi-PUNE (Prop. 3.5).

b. *The solution of* (SR) *is defined by:*

$$X^R(h) = \begin{cases} \hat{X}_0^R + h, & 0 \le h \le h_R \\ \hat{X}_0^R + h_R, & h > h_R \end{cases}$$

where $(\hat{X}_0^R, h_R)$ *is the simultaneous solution of:*

$$\hat{X}_0^R + h^* = \overline{y}, \qquad (3.9c)$$

$$\hat{X}_0^R + \int_0^{h_R} h \, d\mathbf{F}(h) + (1 - F(h_R))h_R = \mu. \qquad (3.9d)$$

We have $\hat{X}_0^R > 0$.

Proposition 3.5 is proved in the Appendix.

Proposition 3.5 is more easily comprehended by studying Figure 3.2, where I graph the solutions X^L and X^R at a point $(h^*, \overline{y}) \in \Gamma$. We indeed see that the constraints (L1) and (R1) in (Q*3a) and (Q*3b) hold, as promised, and so indeed the solutions to programs (SL) and (SR) are quasi-PUNEs.

Note that both policies are fairly simple piece-wise linear policies. The Left proposes to give more to the poor and less to the rich than does the Right, but Left and Right coincide in what they propose for a 'middle class' of voters. The Left proposes a 100 percent marginal tax rate for all types less than h_L and all types greater than h^*, and a zero marginal tax rate for voters in the middle class. The Right proposes a zero marginal tax rate for all voters less than h_R, and a 100 percent marginal tax rate after that. These extreme marginal tax rates are a consequence of the assumption that labor supply is inelastic.

Here is an intuition for the Left's policy solution. Write out the program (SL) in full form:

$$\max_{X} \int_{0}^{h^*} \log X(h)d\mathbf{F}(h)$$

$$s.t.$$

$$\int_{0}^{\infty} X(h)d\mathbf{F}(h) = \mu$$

$$0 \le X'(h) \le 1$$

$$X(h^*) \ge \overline{y}.$$

The graph of the policy must pass through the point $\xi = (h^*, \overline{y})$; subject to this, it must maximize the average welfare of those in $[0, h^*)$. Because utility is concave in X, the Left planner wants to give as much as possible to the poorest in the L coalition. Thus, he gives a high constant amount to as many as possible beginning at $h = 0$; at the last moment, the policy scoots up, as rapidly as allowed, to the point ξ. The 'last moment' is the point h_L at which the policy can ascend at the rate of one and reach ξ. Once having reached ξ, Left should give as little as possible to the citizens in $[h^*, \infty)$. This means the policy must be constant on this interval, as it cannot decrease. Given the point ξ, what Left offers those in the interval $[0, h_L]$, and the value of h_L, are uniquely determined by the budget constraint.

In like manner, we can provide an intuition for Right. By definition, the constraint (R1) is binding, so Right must give total resource $\overline{y}$ to type h^*. To the left of ξ, Right should scoot down as fast as possible – it is a waste to give any resources to those in L, but Right is constrained not to decrease its policy at a rate faster than unity. To the right of ξ, the policy should increase as fast as possible. At some point h_R it must stop, and then it is constrained not to decrease X after that, and so X is constant after h_R. Consequently, the Right's policy has the shape in the graph, and there is a unique such two-piece, piece-wise linear policy that solves the budget constraint.

There is one important fact about these two policies: the graphs of both policies cut the vertical axis *above the origin*, that is, both Left and Right give a positive resource transfer to the type with zero wage capacity.[9] From Figure 3.2, it suffices to show that the Right policy always cuts the vertical axis above the origin. Because the policy can descend from the point ξ at a maximum rate of one, it suffices to show that for all $(h^*, \bar{y}) \in \Gamma$, $\bar{y} > h^*$. From (3.8), it suffices to show that $y^R(h^*) > h^*$. Recall that $y^R(h^*)$ is the value $X(h^*)$, where X is the policy that maximizes $\int_{h^*}^{\infty} \log X(h) d\mathbf{F}(h)$, subject to X in T^*. It is not hard to deduce that this policy gives more than h^* in total resource to h^* (see the Appendix, section 3) and that concludes the argument.

F. ON THE EXISTENCE OF PUNES

There is one particular quasi-PUNE that we can demonstrate is a PUNE. It is, indeed, a PUNE where the Militants of both parties play their ideal policies – that is, the policies that maximize the payoff functions $V^L (V^R)$ on the domain T^*.

Given h^*, define $L = [0, h^*)$ and $R = [h^*, \infty)$. The policies X that maximize V^L and V^R are given by

$$X^L(h) = \mu, \text{ and}$$

$$X^R(h) = \begin{cases} x + h, & \text{if } h \leq y \\ x + y, & \text{if } h > y \end{cases}$$

where (x,y) is the simultaneous solution of

---

[9] Showing that the Right policy gives a positive amount of resources to $h = 0$ is the critical juncture at which we employ the bounds on the derivative of X. If X could increase at rates faster than one, then it would no longer be true that, in quasi-PUNEs, Right always gives positive resources to the poorest citizens. Were this to fail, then the dynamic analysis of Chapter 4 would be quite different: 'poverty traps' could occur from which families would never escape.

$$x + \int_0^y h\, dF(h) + y(1 - F(y)) = \mu \qquad \text{(A3.2a)}$$

$$\int_{h^*}^y \frac{dF(h)}{h+x} = \frac{F(y)}{x+y} \qquad \text{(A3.2b)}$$

respectively. (For proof, see sections 1 and 3 of the Appendix.) If h^* turns out to be indifferent between these two policies (inspection shows that at most one type can be indifferent), then the triple (h^*, X^L, X^R) is indeed a PUNE: for then condition (P3(c)) of the definition of PUNE will hold, and any other policy would decrease the welfare of the Militants of either party (and so no acceptable deviation exists for either party).

In other words, this triple comprises a PUNE exactly when

$$X^R(h^*) = \mu. \qquad (3.10)$$

Equations (3.10), (A3.2a), and (A3.2b) comprise three equations in the unknowns (h^*, x, y) and we proceed to show that they possess a solution.

Theorem 3.1. *Let F be a distribution function of human capital with mean μ, f its density, and $f(0) > 0$. Then there exists a PUNE where both parties play the ideal policies of their Militant factions.*

Proof: We must show that the equations (3.10), (A3.2a), and (A3.2b) possess a solution.

It is easy to see that $x + y > \mu$ always (or else the policy X^R would integrate to less than μ). Therefore equation (3.10) is of the form

$$x + h^* = \mu. \qquad (3.10a)$$

Define the function $Q(y) \equiv \int_0^y h\, dF(h) + y(1 - F(y))$. Then, using (3.10), (3.2), we can eliminate x and h^* from the three-equation system, leaving the single equation:

$$\int_{Q(y)}^{y} \frac{dF(h)}{h + \mu - Q(y)} = \frac{F(y)}{y + \mu - Q(y)}. \tag{3.11}$$

If Equation (3.11) has a solution in y, then we have proved the existence of the stipulated PUNE.

Note that

$$\lim_{y \to \infty} Q(y) = \mu$$

and $Q(0) = 0$.

As y approaches infinity, the r.h.s. of (3.11) approaches zero, while the l.h.s. approaches the number $\int_{\mu}^{\infty} \frac{dF(h)}{h}$, which is *positive*, because, by assumption, **F**'s support is the positive real line. If we can show that there is some value of y for which the l.h.s. of (3.11) is smaller than the r.h.s., then by continuity, there exists a solution to (3.11).

Define the left- and right-hand sides of equation (3.11) as $A(y)$ and $B(y)$, respectively, and compute that

$$B'(y) = \frac{f(y)}{y + \mu - Q(y)} - \left(\frac{F(y)}{y + \mu - Q(y)} \right)^2$$

$$A'(y) = \frac{f(y)}{y + \mu - Q(y)} - \frac{f(Q(y))}{\mu}(1 - F(y))$$

$$+ (1 - F(y)) \int_{Q(y)}^{y} \frac{dF(h)}{(y + \mu - Q(y))^2}.$$

It follows that $B'(0) = \frac{f(0)}{\mu} > 0$ and $A'(0) = \frac{f(0)}{\mu} - \frac{f(0)}{\mu} + 0 = 0$. Note that $A(0) = B(0) = 0$. It follows that for small positive numbers y, $B(y) > A(y)$, which concludes the proof. ∎

We have just demonstrated the existence of a quasi-PUNE on the lower boundary of the manifold Γ where both the L and R parties play the ideal policy of their Militant factions. I call a positive value h^* for which this occurs a *kink*. We do not know that the kink is unique, although typically it will be. (That is, we do not prove that the solution y to Equation (3.11) is unique.)

What matters, for the quasi-PUNEs $(h^*, \overline{y})$ on the lower envelope of the manifold Γ, is whether

$$\overline{y} = y^L(h^*) > y^R(h^*) \qquad \text{(i)}$$

or

$$\overline{y} = y^R(h^*) > y^L(h^*). \qquad \text{(ii)}$$

In case (i), Left plays the ideal policy of its Militants, and Right's Militants compromise, and in case (ii), Right plays the ideal policy of its Militants, and Left's Militants compromise.

The existence of a PUNE where both parties play the ideal policy of their 'average member' is very similar to the main result in Gomberg, Marhenda, and Ortuño-Ortin (2004). They propose a model of political competition with two parties, with a polity whose members have Euclidean preferences on a finite-dimensional policy space. Each party proposes a policy that is the 'ideal' policy of a utility function that is produced by aggregating their members' utility functions in a specified way. As in our model, party membership is stable in the sense that, at equilibrium, no member prefers the policy of the other party. Moreover, in their equilibrium, no coalition (of positive measure) has an incentive to switch parties, taking into account the effect it would have on the other party's utility function.

Although there are a fair number of publications in the literature on political competition in which it is postulated that parties propose the ideal policies of the candidate or the party's members, this assumption is a poor one, and is, I believe, adopted for tractability.[10] As I now discuss, it is difficult to establish, in our model, the existence of PUNEs in which the Militants are not all-powerful.

Let me illustrate why it is difficult to establish whether any other quasi-PUNE is a PUNE. Consider a typical quasi-PUNE, illustrated

---

[10] See, for example, the citizen-candidate model of Osborne and Slivinski (1996) and Besley and Coate (1997).

in Figure 3.2. Call the two policies X^L and X^R. For any policy X define the set:

$$M(X; X^R) = \{h \,|\, X(h) \geq X^R(h)\}.$$

Is there a policy that could defeat X^L, according to criterion (P2) of the definition of PUNE, given X^R? To show this is *not* the case requires showing that X^L solves the following program:

$$\max \int_0^{h^*} \log X(h)\,dF(h)$$

$$s.t. \ X \in T^* \qquad\qquad (3.12)$$

$$\mathbf{F}(M(X; X^R)) \geq F(h^*)$$

In other words: Left's policy should maximize the average welfare of Left's members subject to guaranteeing a vote of at least the same size for Left as X^L achieves. (I ignore here the point that indifferent voters who are members of Right will vote for X^R against X; we could fix this at the cost of an increasingly confusing notation.) Now, unfortunately program (3.12) has a non-convex opportunity set. To see this, let X^1 and X^2 be two feasible points for program (3.12). Pick a value of $\lambda \in (0, 1)$ and consider the policy $X^\lambda \equiv \lambda X^1 + (1 - \lambda)X^2$; this policy dominates X^R on the set $M(X^\lambda; X^R)$. There is no guarantee, however, that $\mathbf{F}(M(X^\lambda; X^R)) \geq F(h^*)$. The operator M is not a concave operator.

Consequently, (3.12) is a non-concave program on an infinite-dimensional space, and the present author cannot provide conditions under which X^L solves it.

We must therefore be content to analyze the dynamics of quasi-PUNEs, a plan that is justified, I hope, by the motivation I provided earlier for the quasi-PUNE concept.

G. TOPPING OFF: PRIVATE VS. PUBLIC EDUCATION

Thus far, we have been assuming that all educational finance is public. We now observe that this assumption is unnecessary.

Will parents wish to augment public investment with private investment in education at the equilibria here? No. The optimizing parent will examine the total resource bundle going to his or her family, $X(h)$. The parent will compute that the optimal partition of this bundle, from the viewpoint of his or her welfare, is exactly the partition that the policy offers: to spend $r(h) = \frac{\gamma c}{1+\gamma c} X(h)$ on education, and $\psi(h) = \frac{1}{1+\gamma c} X(h)$ on consumption. So the parent will not wish to invest either more or less in his or her child's education.

Now suppose that we do not assume that educational investment is public. Each party can offer a platform in which it proposes a policy (ψ, r^{pub}), with the understanding that, if a family is underfunded in education at that public policy, the family will 'top off' the public component with private educational contributions from its after-tax income. We will then have a private educational investment of

$$
r^{pr}(h) = \begin{cases} 0, & \text{if } r^{pub}(h) = \dfrac{\gamma c}{1+\gamma c} X(h) \\[2ex] \dfrac{\gamma c}{1+\gamma c} X(h) - r^{pub}(h), & \text{if } r^{pub}(h) < \dfrac{\gamma c}{1+\gamma c} X(h) \end{cases},
$$

and it is now immediately seen that the parent only cares about $X(h)$, because parental welfare is:

$$
\log(X(h) - r^{pub}(h) - r^{pr}(h)) + \gamma c \log(r^{pr}(h) + r^{pub}(h))
$$
$$
= \log \frac{X(h)}{1+\gamma c} + \gamma c \log \frac{\gamma c X(h)}{1+\gamma c} \cong \log X(h).
$$

(Parties will never propose to spend *more* than parents want on education.) Thus, without loss of generality, the competition between parties again reduces to competition over the total resource bundle, X. Therefore, *the equilibria in a model with public and private education are identical to the equilibria in the model with only public education*: only the mix of public and private financing might change, but there will be no real effects.

We can conclude that our model, as it stands, is incapable of explaining why we have *public* education. It is immaterial to families, here, whether there is public or partially public or entirely private financing of education. Surely, in democratic history, the struggle for public education was extremely important, and so our model is missing an important aspect of history.

In Chapter 5, I will amend the educational production function, and we will then see that the decision to publicly fund education has real consequences. The idea will be to change the environment so that education generates both private and social returns: then it will matter whether the state or families finance education.

H. SUMMARY

We have, in this chapter, modeled political competition between parties that represent two economic classes, over redistribution of income and the educational investment policy. The choice of how to allocate society's resources is taken from an infinite-dimensional policy space of functions, which models the view that competition is ruthless, not being constrained by artificial limitations on the dimension of the policy space. We proposed a slight extension of the PUNE concept, to quasi-PUNE, which, conceptually, is motivated by making the Militant factions even more 'principled' than they are in PUNE. That amendment enabled us to characterize completely the manifold of equilibria in the political game.

We showed that it suffices to study the total-resource functions, X, that are derived from the equilibrium proposals of the parties. In equilibrium, these functions are always piece-wise linear, with at most three segments. Typically, Left gives more to the poor and less to the rich than Right, and typically there is a non-degenerate interval of middle-class families who receive the same from the two parties.

Because there is a two-dimensional equilibrium manifold, we will have to specify particular equilibria if we are to study dynamics. We will concentrate on equilibria that lie on the upper and lower envelopes of the manifold Γ. We pointed out that, at quasi-PUNEs on the upper envelope of the manifold, both parties are as opportunistic as they can be (subject to the existence of a quasi-PUNE); at these points, both parties play the same policy, which is the ideal policy of the pivot individual, h^*. On the lower envelope of the manifold, the parties are as ideological (militant) as they can be. At such points, at least one of the parties is playing the ideal policy of its Militant faction. For large values of h^*, Right's Militants will be playing their ideal policy, and for small values, Left's Militants will be doing so.

We also demonstrated the existence of at least one point on the lower manifold where the Militant factions of both parties play their ideal policy. Such points are also (real) PUNEs. We call values of h^* for which this occurs, kinks.

Finally, we noted that no household would have an incentive to 'top off' public investment in education with private investment. Hence, in the present model, we cannot understand why educational investment is public, and schooling is compulsory. An understanding of that important fact will come from amending the model, as we do in Chapter 5.

CHAPTER 4

The Dynamics of Human Capital with Exogenous Growth

A. THE HOTELLING-DOWNS MODEL

It is instructive to begin the study of dynamics with a much simpler model, that of Hotelling-Downs. This model only (roughly speaking) has an equilibrium when policies are unidimensional.[1] So let us suppose that the policy space is the space of affine total resource functions, that is,

$$X(h) = ah + (1 - a)\mu, \quad 0 \le a \le 1.$$

Here, $1 - a$ is a constant marginal tax rate, and $(1 - a)\mu$ is a lump-sum transfer to all citizens. The utility function and production function are the same as in Chapter 3. As always, consumption and educational investment are divided in proportions $1: \gamma c$. The constraint $a \in [0, 1]$ assures us that X is non-decreasing and has a derivative no larger than one.

Denote the median of the distribution of human capital by m. The indirect utility function of types on policies a now becomes

$$v(a; h) = Log(ah + (1 - a)\mu),$$

which is single-peaked in a. Consequently, because both parties are unremittingly opportunist in the Hotelling-Downs model, the unique

---

[1] For a precise statement, see Roemer (2001, Theorems 6.1 and 6.2).

political equilibrium has them both proposing the ideal policy of the median type, which is

$$a = \begin{cases} 1, & \text{if } m > \mu \\ 0, & \text{if } m < \mu \end{cases}.$$

That is, if the median is less than the mean, $X(h) = \mu$, while if the median is greater than the mean, then $X(h) = h$, the laissez-faire policy.

Let us begin with a distribution in which median human capital is less than mean human capital. Suppose as well that $b + c = 1$. Then the policy $X(h) = \mu$ is played by both parties, and wins. This generates a distribution of human capital at date 1. As long as, at date t, $m^t < \mu^t$, there will be constant investment in all children, and if this continues forever, then we converge to *equality of wages*, in the sense of a zero coefficient of variation of human capital, because the ratio of wages of any two dynasties approaches unity. Indeed, we have, if $S(h)$ is the human capital of the son of h, and $h_2 > h_1$, then:

$$\frac{S(h_2)}{S(h_1)} = \frac{h_2^b \mu^{1-b}}{h_1^b \mu^{1-b}} = \left(\frac{h_2}{h_1}\right)^b,$$

and after t dates where the median is less than the mean:

$$\frac{S^t(h_2)}{S^t(h_1)} = \left(\frac{h_2}{h_1}\right)^{b^t},$$

where $S^t(h)$ is the human capital of the tth descendent of h.

On the other hand, if there is some date at which the median is greater than the mean, then the laissez-faire distribution is implemented, and the distribution of human capital remains unchanged thereafter (here, invoke $b + c = 1$). Therefore the median is greater than the mean at the next date, and so on forever. Thus, if the median is ever greater than the mean, then the coefficient of variation is constant and positive forever after.

Our question thus becomes: when is it the case that the median is less than the mean forever under this sequence of policies?

Define, for any distribution function F:

$$\rho(F) = \int \log h \, dF(h).$$

Theorem 4.1. *Let $b + c = 1$. Let F be the date 0 distribution of h, with median m and mean μ. Under Hotelling-Downs politics, on the unidimensional policy space of affine functions, the coefficient of variation of the distribution of human capital (CVHC) converges to zero if and only if*

$$\log m \leq \rho(F).$$

To prove the theorem, we use a well-known fact from analysis:

Lemma 4.1. *For any distribution function, define $M_r = (\int h^r \, dF(h))^{\frac{1}{r}}$. Then:*

(a) *As r approaches zero from above, M_r is decreasing;*
(b) $\lim_{r \to 0} M_r = \exp[\rho(F)]$.

Proof: See, for example, Hardy, Littlewood, and Pólya (1964).   ∎

Proof of Theorem 4.1: We have observed that convergence to equality occurs if and only if, for all t, the median m^t is less than the mean μ^t. (Equality of the mean and median is a singularity that we ignore; in that case, there is a continuum of equilibrium policies.) In period t, if the median has been less than the mean in all prior periods, the median and mean of the distribution are given by

$$km^{b^t} \quad \text{and} \quad k \int h^{b^t} \, dF(h),$$

respectively, for some constant k. We wish, therefore, to know if:

$$m^r < \int h^r \, dF(h)$$

where $r = b^t$; in other words, whether

$$m < \left(\int h^r \, dF(h) \right)^{\frac{1}{r}} \equiv M_r(F). \tag{4.1}$$

Now $b < 1$ implies that r decreases to zero as t gets larger. From lemma 4.1, it follows that inequality (4.1) is true for all $t \geq 0$ iff $m \leq \exp(\int \log h \, dF(h))$, or, in other words iff

$$\log m \leq \rho(F).$$

This is therefore precisely the condition in which the CVHC tends to be zero.   ■

The condition "$\log m \leq \int \log h \, dF(h)$" is stronger than the condition "$m \leq \mu$." (Just note that $\log m \leq \int \log h \, dF(h) \Rightarrow m \leq \exp(\int \log h \, dF(h)) \Rightarrow m \leq \int h \, dF(h) = \mu$, where the last implication follows from Jensen's inequality.) But the converse direction is generally false. So the critical inequality for the theorem is one that can be interpreted as *strong positive skewness* of the distribution F (because '$m < \mu$' is commonly called *positive skewness*).

The lognormal distribution satisfies precisely the equation

$$\log m = \int \log h \, dF(h).$$

So, if the initial distribution is lognormal, wages will converge to equality under Hotelling-Downs.

We will see that the number $\rho(F)$ plays a key role in our problem on the infinite-dimensional policy space.

B. SOME SIMPLE DYNAMICS IN THE INFINITE-DIMENSIONAL CASE

Let us examine what would happen under laissez-faire, a regime with no taxation or redistribution, where $X(h) = h$, and where each parent invests privately in the education of his or her child. Educational investment would be

$$r(h) = \frac{\gamma c h}{1 + \gamma c},$$

and substituting this into the educational production function yields the future wage of the child as:

$$h' = \alpha h^b r(h)^c = \alpha \left(\frac{\gamma c}{1 + \gamma c} \right)^c h^{b+c}.$$

Hence the ratio of wages of the children from parents whose wages are $h_1 > h_2$ is $(\frac{h_1}{h_2})^{b+c}$. Thus, at the end of the tth generation, the wage ratio of the two dynasties is $(\frac{h_1}{h_2})^{(b+c)^t}$. This number approaches one, is constant, or explodes, as returns to scale are decreasing, constant, or increasing, respectively. That is, if returns to scale are decreasing, then, even under laissez-faire, the ratio of the wages in any two dynasties approaches unity, and so it follows that the coefficient of variation of the distribution of human capital approaches zero. We say that *wages tend to equality* if the coefficient of variation of that distribution approaches zero. If returns to scale are constant, then the coefficient of variation is constant through time, with laissez-faire.

By adopting the coefficient of variation rather than the variance as the measure of wage dispersion, we show a concern for the ratios of wages rather than their differences.

We next examine what happens with equilibrium policies in our model. We first observe:

Proposition 4.1. *Let* (X^L, X^R) *be any quasi-PUNE.*
Let $(h_1, X(h_1))$ *and* $(h_2, X(h_2))$ *be two points on the graph of either policy (i.e., X can be either X^L or X^R). Then the line containing these two points intersects the ordinate axis above the origin. Formally,*

$$\frac{X(h_1)}{h_1} > \frac{X(h_2) - X(h_1)}{h_2 - h_1}.$$

This proposition is clear from examining Figure 3.2. It follows from observing that both policies themselves cut the vertical axis above the origin, and that their slopes are never greater than one.

Let X be an equilibrium policy in a quasi-PUNE, and let $h_2 > h_1$. Then the educational investment is $r(h) = \frac{\gamma c X(h)}{1+\gamma c}$. Let the chord through the points $(h_1, X(h_1))$ and $(h_2, X(h_2))$ have the equation $x = mh + d$; we know that m is non-negative and d is positive by Proposition 4.1. Then we can write the wage of the son of h_i as:

$$h_i' = \alpha h_i^b \left(\frac{\gamma c}{1+\gamma c}(mh_i + d)\right)^c, \quad i = 1, 2$$

and so the ratio of wages of the two dynasties at the first generation is:

$$\frac{h_2'}{h_1'} = \left(\frac{h_2}{h_1}\right)^b \left(\frac{mh_2 + d}{mh_1 + d}\right)^c < \left(\frac{h_2}{h_1}\right)^{b+c},$$

where the strict inequality follows from the fact that $d > 0$. Thus, with decreasing returns to scale, wages tend to equality, regardless of which party wins which election at each date. And even with constant returns to scale, the wage ratios of any rich dynasty to any poor dynasty decrease monotonically over time. Whether they decrease to unity or not will determine whether or not wages tend to equality.

In reality, what are the returns to scale in the educational production function? In Chapter 6, we study this question. For now, I want to observe that *if* the returns to scale are decreasing ($b + c < 1$), then both laissez-faire and democracy will eventually produce equality of wages. To distinguish between the behavior of these two regimes – and I wish to take laissez-faire as the benchmark – we would have to study *speeds of convergence* of the coefficient of variation to zero, and this is a delicate undertaking. On the other hand, with constant returns ($b + c = 1$), a sharp distinction obtains: under laissez-faire, the coefficient of variation is constant, while under democracy, it is monotone decreasing.

My strategy will be to study the dynamic process when $b + c = 1$. If we can show that wages tend to equality in this case, then we have confidence in saying that, even if $b + c < 1$, wages will converge faster to equality with democracy than with laissez-faire, but if wages do not tend to equality with constant returns, then we cannot make such a statement.

There is a second – and perhaps major – reason to concentrate on the case $b + c = 1$: in this case only, the distribution of human capital remains stationary under the laissez-faire policy, while if $b + c < 1$, then human capitals converge to equality even under laissez-faire. Therefore, by studying the case of constant returns we focus upon the effect of *political competition* on the distribution of human capital rather than the effect of *technology*. This is, indeed, the task of our study: to understand the extent to which *democracy* will, over time, account for a tendency to economic equality.

In sum, our next task is to study the ratio of wages in pairs of dynasties over time, under the assumption that $b + c = 1$. Do wages tend to equality under democracy with ruthless competition?

C. QUASI-PUNE DYNAMICS

We have observed that, if there are constant returns to scale ($b + c = 1$) then, under laissez-faire, the distribution of human capital remains constant over time except for a multiplicative growth factor. On the other hand, if at every period educational finance is determined by a political equilibrium (quasi-PUNE), then, regardless of which party wins the election, the coefficient of variation of the distribution of human capital is strictly monotone decreasing. Our task, now, is to study whether that coefficient of variation tends to some positive number, or to zero.

It is convenient, for the moment, to normalize the distributions of human capital that occur over time to have constant mean. Thus, if $\mathbf{F}^t$ is the probability distribution of human capital at date $t, t = 0, 1, \ldots,$ and its mean is μ^t define the normalized distributions

$$\hat{F}^t(h) = F^t \left(\frac{\mu^0}{\mu^t} h \right), \tag{4.2}$$

which all have mean μ^0. This transformation does not affect the coefficients of variation of the distributions, so it suffices to study the dynamics of the coefficients of variation of the sequence $\{\hat{F}^t\}$.

Denote the coefficient of variation of $\hat{F}^t$ by η^t.

Our first observation is:

Proposition 4.2. *Let $b + c \leq 1$. Then*

(a) *the distribution function $\hat{F}^{t+1}$ cuts the distribution function $\hat{F}^t$ once from below. That is,*

$$(\exists h')(0 < h < h' \Rightarrow \hat{F}^{t+1}(h) < \hat{F}^t(h) \quad and$$
$$h > h' \Rightarrow \hat{F}^{t+1}(h) > \hat{F}^{t+1}(h)).$$

(b) *$\hat{F}^{t+1}$ second-order stochastic dominates $\hat{F}^t$.*

(c) *The sequence $\{\eta^t\}$ is monotone decreasing, and hence converges.*

Proof: See Appendix.   ∎

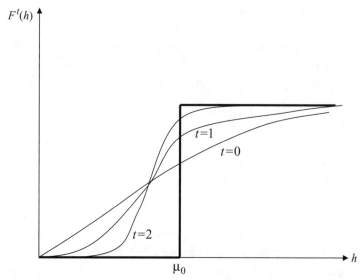

Figure 4.1. The normalized CDF of human capital at various dates.

We have already observed part (c). Part (b) follows from part (a). Part (a) is proved by again exploiting the fact that both educational investment functions give a positive investment to families at the lowest level of human capital.

Part (a) of the proposition is illustrated in Figure 4.1. What is not yet clear is whether these CDFs converge to the one with all its mass at the mean, indicated by the heavy line in the figure, or if the convergence stops before that.

Consider the manifold of quasi-PUNEs, illustrated in Figure 3.1. Fix a pivot type h^* at which the probability of victory is positive for both parties. At any quasi-PUNE with h^* as the pivot, those who (are expected to) vote Left are in the interval $[0, h^*)$; hence the probability of Left victory is $\frac{1}{2} + \frac{F(h^*) - \frac{1}{2}}{2\beta}$, where β is the error term (see Chapter 2). Because the educational investment function is weakly monotone increasing, whichever party wins, it follows that the mapping of parent's human capital to child's human capital is *strictly* increasing, and so descendents occupy exactly the same rank in their distribution of human capital as their ancestors. Let $S^t(h^*)$ be the human capital of the tth descendent of h^*. It follows that

$$\hat{F}^t(S^t(h^*)) = F^0(h^*).$$

Let us therefore fix a sequence of quasi-PUNEs in which, at every date, the pivot type is the descendent of our given h^* from date zero. Then the probabilities of Left victory will be constant in the sequence.

Our dynamic analysis will investigate two such sequences. One sequence is denoted $B(h^*)$, where the pivot is $S^t(h^*)$ at date t and the quasi-PUNE lies on the lower boundary of the equilibrium manifold. The other sequence, denoted $A(h^*)$, again has the pivot as the tth descendent of h^*, but it lies on the upper boundary of the manifold. Recall from Chapter 3 that the B sequence is one where politics are *ideological*, in the sense that the Militants are as powerful as they can be in the intra-party bargaining game, and the A sequence is one in which politics are *opportunist*.

We have:

Theorem 4.2. *Let $b + c = 1$, and let F be the initial distribution of human capital. Let $h^* > 0$ be any pivot at which both parties win with positive probability. Then the limit of the CVHC in the A-sequence of quasi-PUNEs is positive.*

Thus opportunist politics *never* engender equality of human capital in the long run; the story is clearly different from that of the Hotelling-Downs model (Theorem 4.1).

Let me attempt to motivate the result, which is proved in the Appendix.

In the sequence $A(h^*)$, both parties play the ideal policy of the *pivot* voter, which is graphed in Figure 4.2. Because investment is constant for $h > h^*$, it follows that, over time, the ratio of the human capitals of any two dynasties $h_1 > h_2$ that are greater than h^* approaches one. This is because their ratio at date t is simply $(\frac{h_1}{h_2})^{b^t}$, which approaches one, because $b < 1$. The question is what happens to the ratios of human capital in dynasties that are smaller than h^*?

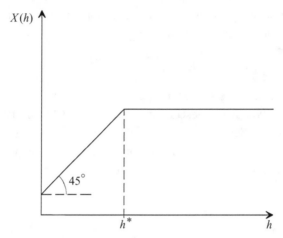

Figure 4.2. The policy played by both parties on the upper boundary of manifold Γ.

Suppose that the educational investment function illustrated in figure 4.2 passed through the origin, instead of above it. Then, on the interval $[0, h^*)$, the investment function would be exactly the laissez-faire investment function, and hence the distribution of human capital in that interval would stay the same over time. Thus, intuitively, the issue is: how rapidly does the vertical intercept of the investment function approach the origin? (It does approach the origin.) The proof shows that the intercept approaches the origin 'fast,' and so the coefficient of variation of the distribution stays bounded away from zero. Indeed, it converges to a positive number.

Of course, the distributions of human capital need not converge to a distribution: there could be constant growth. But the *mean-normalized distribution functions* do indeed converge to a distribution function.

What happens in a *B*-sequence, under ideological politics? I have been unable to resolve the problem completely. I present what I know, and offer some conjectures based on simulations.

It will be useful to name the four policies that can occur on the lower envelope of the quasi-PUNE manifold Γ at a given date. As we have shown in Chapter 3, the policies of the Left and Right parties depend upon whether case (i) or case (ii) (see page 59 of Chapter 3) hold. In case (i), the Left plays the ideal policy of its Militants, and the

Right compromises; in case (ii), the Right plays the ideal policy of its Militants, and the Left must compromise.

We remind the reader of the definition of the truncated mean function, introduced in the proof of Theorem 3.1:

$$Q(y) = \int_0^y h \, dF(h) + y(1 - F(y)) = \int_0^\infty \min[h, y] dF(h).$$

Note that $Q(\infty) = \mu$ and that Q is an increasing function.

We here re-state, with a somewhat different notation, what we derived in Chapter 3. If case (i) holds, then the Left policy is given by

$$X^L(h) \equiv \mu,$$

and the Right policy is given by

$$X^R(h) = \begin{cases} h + x_2, & \text{if } h \le y_2 \\ y_2 + x_2, & \text{if } h > y_2 \end{cases} = x_2 + \min[h, y_2]$$

where (x_2, y_2) solves:

$$x_2 + Q(y_2) = \mu \tag{4.3a}$$
$$x_2 + h^* = \mu. \tag{4.3b}$$

Note that (4.3a) says that X^R integrates to μ, while (4.3b) says that $X^R(h^*) = X^L(h^*)$, a necessary condition for all quasi-PUNEs.

If case (ii) holds, then Right plays the ideal policy of its Militants, which is:

$$Y^R(h) = \begin{cases} x_1 + h, & \text{if } h \le y_1 \\ x_1 + y_1, & \text{if } h > y_1 \end{cases} = x_1 + \min[h, y_1]$$

where (x_1, y_1) solves:

$$\int_{h^*}^{y_1} \frac{dF(h)}{h + x_1} = \frac{F(y_1)}{y_1 + x_1} \tag{4.4a}$$

$$x_1 + Q(y_1) = \mu \tag{4.4b}$$

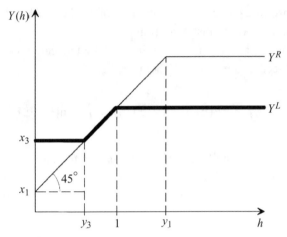

Figure 4.3. Policies at $B(h^*)$ when left must compromise (case (ii)).

and Left plays the policy:

$$Y^L(h) = \begin{cases} x_3, & \text{if } h \leq y_3 \\ x_3 + h - y_3, & \text{if } y_3 < h \leq h^* \\ x_3 + h^* - y_3, & \text{if } h > h^* \end{cases}$$

where (x_3, y_3) solves:

$$x_3 + Q(h^*) - Q(y_3) = \mu \qquad (4.5a)$$
$$x_3 - y_3 = x_1 \qquad (4.5b)$$

where (4.5a) says that the policy integrates to μ, and (4.5b) says that $Y^L(h^*) = Y^R(h^*)$. See Figure 4.3 for the graphs of Y^L and Y^R.

We fix a pivot h^* on the lower envelope. In what follows, *we normalize the distribution at each date by setting the pivot equal to unity.* (This does not disturb the coefficients of variation of the distributions.) Thus, if h is the human capital of the parent and the policy X is victorious, then the human capital of the child will be, after the normalization:

$$S(h) = \frac{\alpha h^b \left(\frac{\gamma c}{1+\gamma c} X(h)\right)^{1-b}}{\alpha 1^b \left(\frac{\gamma c}{1+\gamma c} X(1)\right)^{1-b}} = h^b \left(\frac{X(h)}{X(1)}\right)^{1-b}. \qquad (4.6)$$

Because the distribution function at date $t+1$ preserves the rank order of every dynasty, it is defined from the distribution function at date t by

$$F^{t+1}(S(h)) = F^t(h).$$

Thus, F^{t+1} is the function defined by the set of ordered pairs $\{(h^b(\frac{X(h)}{X(1)})^{1-b}, F^t(h)) \mid 0 \le h < \infty\}$.

We fix $0 < b < 1$.

Proposition 4.3. *Let $\{F^t\}$ be a B-sequence of distribution functions where the pivot (the current member of the h^* dynasty) is always normalized to one. Then $\{F^t\}$ converges to a distribution function F^*.*

Proof:

1. We have observed in Chapter 3 that x_1, x_2, and x_3 are all positive and that $y_1 > 1$, $y_2 > 1$, and $y_3 < 1$.

2. We claim that for all four policies named here, we have:

   $$h < 1 \Rightarrow S(h) > h$$
   $$h > 1 \Rightarrow S(h) < h.$$

   By equation (4.6) it suffices to show that:

   $$h < 1 \Rightarrow X(h) > hX(1)$$
   $$h > 1 \Rightarrow X(h) < hX(1)$$

   where X denotes any of the four policies. Let us verify this for Y^R. If $h < 1$, then $Y^R(h) = x_1 + h$ and $Y^R(1) = x_1 + 1$, from which the required inequality follows, because $x_1 > 0$. The other demonstrations are equally straightforward and are left to the reader.

3. It follows that, for any B-sequence, and any $0 < h < 1$, $\{S^t(h)\}$ is a strictly monotone increasing sequence, bounded above by one; hence it converges to a limit point.

Similarly, for any $h > 1$, $\{S^t(h)\}$ is a strictly monotone decreasing sequence bounded below by one, and so converges to a limit point.

Because $F^t(h) = F^{t+1}(S(h))$, we have

$$F^{t+1}(h) < F^t(h), \quad \text{for } h < 1$$
$$F^{t+1}(h) > F^t(h), \quad \text{for } h > 1$$

and so $\lim_{t \to \infty} F^t(h)$ exists for all h. We define this limit to be $F^*(h)$, the limit distribution. ■

The coefficient of variation of human capital (CVHC) converges to zero in a B-sequence if and only if F^* is the degenerate distribution that places all the mass at unity: that is, iff

$$F^*(h) = \begin{cases} 0, & \text{if } h < 1 \\ 1, & \text{if } h \geq 1 \end{cases}.$$

We denote the point-mass distribution function by E for 'egalitarian.'

Proposition 4.4. *Let* $\{F^t\}$ *be any B-sequence of distributions such that*

(1) $\rho(F^t) \geq 0$ *for all* t,
(2) *Left wins an infinite number of times.*

Then $F^* = E$.

Proof:

1. Because F^0 has support $\mathbf{R}_+$, so does F^t for all t.
2. By Jensen's inequality:

    $$0 \leq \rho(F^t) < \log \int_0^\infty h \, dF^t(h) = \log \mu^t,$$

    and so $\mu^t > 1$ for all t. The strict inequality uses the fact that F^t is not the point mass.
3. Because, for all $h > 1$:

    $$X_1^L(h) = X_1^L(1) \quad \text{and} \quad X_2^L(h) = X_2^L(1)$$

    and because Left wins an infinite number of times, and because $h > 1$ implies that $S(h) < h$ when Right wins, we know that F^* possesses no mass above one (that is, $F^*(1) = 1$). It therefore follows that $\mu^* \leq 1$, where $\mu^* = \text{mean } F^*$.

4. But $\mu^t > 1$ for all t implies that $\mu^* \geq 1$, therefore $\mu^* = 1$.

5. It follows that *all* the mass of F^* lies at one (because there is no mass above one, so none can lie below one). Hence $F^* = E$.   ■

Proposition 4.5. *Let $\{F^t\}$ be a B-sequence, where F^0 has support $\mathbf{R}_+$. Then:*

(1) $\rho(F^{t+1}) = b\rho(F^t)$ *if X^L is the winning policy at date t, and*

(2) $\rho(F^{t+1}) < b\rho(F^t)$ *in case any of the other three policies is enacted.*

Proof:

1. If X^L is the winning policy at date t, then

$$\rho(F^{t+1}) = \int \log S(h)\, dF^t(h) = \int \log h^b\, dF^t(h) = b\rho(F^t).$$

2. Consider the case when the winning policy at date t, X, is not X^L. Then:

$$\rho(F^{t+1}) = \int \log S(h)\, dF^t(h) = \int \log h^b \left(\frac{X(h)}{X(1)}\right)^{1-b} dF^t(h)$$

$$= b \int \log h\, dF^t(h)$$

$$+ (1-b)\left\{\int \log X(h) dF^t(h) - \log X(1)\right\}$$

$$= b\rho(F^t) + (1-b)\left\{\int \log X(h) dF^t(h) - \log X(1)\right\}$$

$$(4.7)$$

Note that $X^R(1) = \mu$ and $Y^L(1) = Y^R(1) > \mu$ and so $X(1) \geq \mu$ and $\log X(1) \geq \log \mu$. On the other hand,

$$\int \log X(h) dF^t(h) < \log \int X(h) dF^t(h) = \log \mu, \qquad (4.8)$$

by invoking Jensen's inequality, and the fact that the support of F^t is the positive real line. It follows that the term in brackets in the last line of equation (4.7) is negative, and so $\rho(F^{t+1}) < b\rho(F^t)$ as claimed.   ■

Proposition 4.6. *Let* $\{F^t\}$ *be a B-sequence; denote* $\mu^t = mean\, F^t$. *Then* $\mu^{t+1} \leq \mu^t$ *for all* t.

Proof:

1. Let us view μ^{t+1} as a function of b:

$$\mu^{t+1}(b) = \int S(h) dF^t(h) = \int h^b \left(\frac{X(h)}{X(1)} \right)^{1-b} dF^t(h).$$

Differentiating $\mu^{t+1}(\cdot)$ twice (with respect to b) produces the second derivative:

$$D^2 \mu^{t+1}(b) = \int S(h)(\log h + \log X(1) - \log X(h))^2 dF^t(h).$$

Because the integrand is non-negative (and almost everywhere positive), $\mu^{t+1}(\cdot)$ is a convex function, and hence achieves its maximum on the interval $[0,1]$ at one of the endpoints.

2. Evaluate

$$\mu^{t+1}(0) = \int \frac{X(h)}{X(1)} dF^t(h) = \frac{\mu^t}{X(1)}.$$

If at date $t, h^* = 1$ was on the left branch of the lower envelope, then $X(1) = X^R(1) = x_2 + 1 > 1$. If at date $t, h^* = 1$ was on the right branch, then $X(1) = Y^R(1) = x_1 + 1 > 1$. It follows that $\mu^{t+1}(0) < \mu^t$.

On the other hand, $\mu^{t+1}(1) = \int h\, dF^t(h) = \mu^t$. Therefore, from step 1,

$$\mu^t = \max_{\beta \in [0,1]} \mu^{t+1}(\beta)$$

and so, for our *particular* value of b, we have $\mu^{t+1} = \mu^{t+1}(b) \leq \mu^t$. ∎

Proposition 4.7. *Suppose* $\rho(F^0) < 0$. *Let* $\{F^t\}$ *be a B-sequence in which Left wins an infinite number of times. Then* $F^* \neq E$.

Proof:

1. We first assume that Left wins every election.

If X^L wins at date t, then $S(h) = h^b$. If Y^L wins, then

$$
S(h) = \begin{cases}
h^b \left(\dfrac{x_3}{x_3 + 1 - y_3} \right)^{1-b}, & \text{if } h \le y_3 \\[2ex]
h^b \left(\dfrac{x_3 + h - y_3}{x_3 + 1 - y_3} \right)^{1-b}, & \text{if } y_3 \le h \le 1 \\[2ex]
h^b, & \text{if } h > 1
\end{cases}
$$

Check that in all three cases, $S(h) \le h^b$. Therefore, regardless of which Left policy wins, $S(h) \le h^b$ and so, for any date, $S^t(h) \le h^{b^t}$.

2. Therefore $\mu^t = \int S^t(h)\, dF^0(h) \le \int h^{b^t} dF^0(h)$.
    By lemma 4.1 and because $\exp \rho(F^0) < 1$, we know that, for large t,

$$
\left(\int h^{b^t} dF^0(h) \right)^{\frac{1}{b^t}} < 1.
$$

Therefore, for large t, $\left(\int h^{b^t} dF^0(h) \right) < 1$, and so $\mu^t < 1$.

3. Now invoke Proposition 4.6: because $\{\mu^t\}$ is a decreasing sequence, it must be that $\lim_{t \to \infty} \mu^t < 1$. Hence $F^* \ne E$.

4. We now relax the assumption that Left wins every election. If Left wins t elections in a row, then $S^t(h) \le h^{b^t}$. Now suppose that Right wins n elections in a row. If $h > 1$, we know that $S^{t+n}(h) < h^{b^t}$, because the human capital of $h > 1$ decreases under all four policies. Hence we know that after T Left victories, consecutive or not, the human capital of the descendent of h is less than h^{b^T}. On the other hand, for $h < 1$, if Right wins, then $S(h) = h^b \left(\frac{h+x}{1+x} \right)^{1-b} < h^b$ because $\left(\frac{h+x}{1+x} \right)^{1-b} < 1$. So in both cases, after T Left victories, consecutive or not, we have that the current member of the h dynasty has human capital less than or equal to h^{b^T}.

Hence the argument of steps 2 and 3 continues to apply, and $F^* \ne E$.

∎

We thus have:

Theorem 4.3. *Let $\{F^t\}$ be a B-sequence in which Left wins an infinite number of times. Then $F^* = E$ if and only if $\rho(F^t) \ge 0$ for all t.*

Proof: Immediate consequence of propositions 4.4 and 4.7.   ■

Clearly, Theorem 4.3 is a generalization to the infinite-dimensional case of Theorem 4.1. Recall that, by the normalization, $h^* = 1$ always, so $\log h^* = 0$.

Proposition 4.8. *Let $\rho(F^0) = 0$. Then with probability one, $F^* \neq E$.*

Proof: From Proposition 4.5, at the first Right victory, date t, we will have $\rho(F^t) < 0$. Right wins at least once, with probability one. Now apply Theorem 4.3; with probability one, Left wins an infinite number of times, so the theorem applies.   ■

Proposition 4.9. *Let $\rho(F^0) > 0$. If b is sufficiently small, then if Right wins the first election, $\rho(F^1) < 0$.*

Proof: This follows immediately from the first step of the proof of Proposition 4.5. There it was shown that $\rho(F^{t+1}) = b\rho(F^t) + (1 - b)Neg$ where Neg is a negative number, if Right wins at date t. The claim follows.   ■

These results summarize what I can prove about the stochastic process $B(h^*)$. The difficult problem, thus far unsolved, is to characterize the probability that $\rho(F^t) \geq 0$ for all t.

In the next two sections, I report results of simulations to determine the nature of convergence to equality of human capital.

D. SIMULATIONS OF DYNAMICS OF $B(h^*)$
FOR A DISCRETE DISTRIBUTION

To better understand the dynamics of the process $B(h^*)$, where the equilibrium lies on the lower boundary of the manifold, I analyze that process beginning with a distribution whose mass lies entirely at three discrete points. The reason to study a discrete distribution is that the distribution function can be computed precisely at each date of the dynamic process, and the simulations are carried out rapidly. It is much

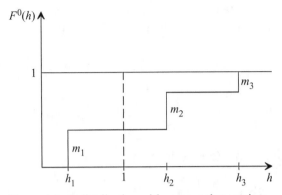

Figure 4.4. A distribution with mass at three points.

more difficult to achieve accurate simulation results beginning with a continuous distribution: that is the topic of the next section of this chapter.

For the remainder of this section, I take $b = 0.5$, and begin with a distribution F^0, illustrated in Figure 4.4, given by:

$$F^0(h) = \begin{cases} 0, & \text{if } h < h_1 \\ m_1, & \text{if } h_1 \le h < h_2 \\ m_1 + m_2, & \text{if } h_2 \le h < h_3 \\ 1, & \text{if } h \ge h_3 \end{cases}$$

where $h_1 < 1 < h_2 < h_3$ and $m_1 + m_2 + m_3 = 1$. Thus

$$\rho(F^0) = \sum m_i \log h_i.$$

We shall choose F^0 so that $\rho(F^0) > 0$ and so $\mu^0 > 1$.

Right must compromise at a quasi-PUNE on the lower envelope if and only if

$$x_1 + 1 < \mu,$$

which, by (4.4b), means that $Q(y_1) > 1$.

We now solve for the parameters necessary to characterize the four policies X^L, X^R, Y^L, and Y^R. Clearly, $X^L(h) \equiv \mu$.

Compute that

$$h_3 \ge y \ge h_2 \Rightarrow Q(y) = m_1 h_1 + m_2 h_2 + m_3 y.$$

An easy way to see this: $Q(y)$ is just the area above the distribution function, bounded above by the line $F = 1$, and bounded on the right by the line $h = y$.

Thus the two equations (4.4a, 4.4b) become in the discrete case:

$$\frac{m_2}{x_1 + h_2} = \frac{m_1 + m_2}{x_1 + y_1},$$
$$x_1 + m_1 h_1 + m_2 h_2 + m_3 y_1 = \mu$$

assuming that $y_1 < h_3$. These solve to give:

$$x_1^* = m_3(h_3 - y_1)$$
$$y_1^* = \frac{h_2(1 - m_3) + m_1 m_3 h_3}{m_2 + m_1 m_3}.$$

We compute that $y_1 < h_3$ if and only if $h_2(1 - m_3) < m_2 h_3$. Hence the complete definition of (x_1, y_1) is:

$$
\begin{cases}
x_1 = \begin{cases} m_3(h_3 - y_1), & \text{if } h_2(1 - m_3) < m_2 h_3 \\ 0, & \text{otherwise} \end{cases} \\[2ex]
y_1 = \begin{cases} y_1^*, & \text{if } h_2(1 - m_3) < m_2 h_3 \\ h_3, & \text{otherwise.} \end{cases}
\end{cases}
\tag{4.9}
$$

To characterize X^R, we write the discrete versions of equations (4.3a, 4.3b):

$$x_2 = \mu - 1 \tag{4.10a}$$

$$
y_2 = \begin{cases}
\dfrac{1 - (m_1 h_1 + m_2 h_2)}{m_3}, & \text{if } m_3 h_2 < 1 - (m_1 h_1 + m_2 h_2) \\[2ex]
\dfrac{1 - m_1 h_1}{1 - m_1}, & \text{otherwise.}
\end{cases}
$$

$$\tag{4.10b}$$

The bifurcated formula for y_2 is necessary because of two possible cases, that y_2 turns out to be greater or less than h_2. Because these equations apply when $Q(y_1) \geq 1$, and so $\mu \geq 1$, we have $x_2 \geq 0$ and $y_2 \leq h_3$, as required.

To solve for Y^L we need to write the discrete versions of (4.5a, 4.5b). Equation (4.5b) remains as is, while (4.5a) expands to

$$x_3 + \int_{y_3}^{1} h\, dF(h) + (1 - y_3)(1 - F(1)) = \mu.$$

The discrete version of the last equation depends on whether $y_3 \gtrless h_1$. It can be shown that $y_3 > h_1$ always. Therefore, $\int_{y_3}^{1} h\, dF(h) = 0$ and the above equation implies that:

$$y_3 = \frac{\mu - x_1 - 1 + m_1}{m_1},$$

invoking $F(1) = m_1$.

We have solved for the four policies in the discrete case illustrated in Figure 4.4. We now describe the simulations. For simplicity, we assume that the probability of Left victory is, at each date, m_1 which is always equal to $F^t(1)$, the (expected) vote share of Left. The distribution function at date t is given by

$$\text{mass } m_i \text{ at } S^t(h_i), \quad i = 1, 2, 3.$$

At each date, we compute $Q(y_1)$. We define a variable

$$\sigma = \begin{cases} 1, & \text{if } Q(y_1) \geq 1 \\ 0, & \text{otherwise} \end{cases}.$$

We randomly choose a winner of the election, which will be Left with probability m_1, and define:

$$\delta = \begin{cases} 1, & \text{if Left wins} \\ 0, & \text{if Right wins} \end{cases}.$$

We implement the policy

$$X(h) = \delta(\sigma X^L(h) + (1 - \sigma)Y^L(h)) $$
$$+ (1 - \delta)(\sigma X^R(h) + (1 - \sigma)Y^R(h)).$$

We then compute the values $\{S(h_i) \mid i = 1, 2, 3\}$ according to the formula $S(h) = h^b(\frac{X(h)}{X(1)})^{1-b}$. Finally we replace h_i with $S(h_i)$ and repeat the procedure fifty times (i.e., for fifty generations). At each iteration, we compute $\rho(F^t)$.

Table 4.1. *Simulations of distributions with three mass points.*

Collection #	m_1	m_2	m_3	h_1	h_2	h_3	$\rho(F^0)$	prob. of conv.
1	.5	.3	.2	.5	1.3	20	.331	16.5%
2	.6	.2	.2	.5	1.3	7	.026	3.2%
3	.3	.5	.2	.5	1.3	7.	.312	0.12%
4	.8	.1	.1	.5	1.3	200.	.0016	7.7%
5	.5	.3	.2	.5	1.3	10^4	.393	55.2%
6	.5	.3	.2	.5	1.3	10^6	.853	67.2%
7	.5	.3	.2	.5	1.3	10^9	3.88	75.7%
8	.5	.3	.2	.9	4.	10^8	4.05	96%

We know, because in an infinite history Left wins an infinite number of times, with probability one, that $S^t(h_2) \to 1$ and $S^t(h_3) \to 1$. The only question is whether $S^t(h_1) \to 1$. We declare that convergence to equality occurs in a simulation if $S^{50}(h_1) > 1 - 10^{-7}$. Of course, we can also check whether $\rho(F^t) > 0$ for all t, and refer to Theorem 4.3.

What we learn from the simulations is that the probability of convergence to equality depends intimately on the size of $\rho(F^t)$ and the magnitude of m_1. Call one simulation of fifty generations a *history*. Call a super-iteration of 5,000 histories, all of the same stochastic process, a *collection* of histories. For each collection of histories, I computed the fraction of histories within it that converge to equality. For example, defining F^0 by

$$(m_1, m_2, m_3) = (0.5, 0.3, 0.2), (h_1, h_2, h_3) = (0.5, 1.3, 20),$$

and taking $b = 0.5$, we have $\rho(F^0) = 0.331$. The fraction of histories that converged to equality in the collection was 16.5 percent. We can confidently assert that convergence to equality occurs with positive probability, significantly less than one.

Table 4.1 reports the probability of convergence to equality, so derived, for several choices of the initial distribution.

What appears to be the case is that the probability of convergence is increasing in m_1 and in $\rho(F^0)$. Runs 7 and 8 are interesting; they establish the importance of the value of $\rho(F^0)$ as opposed to the mean of the initial distribution: the Run 8 distribution dominates Run 7 in terms of $\rho(F^0)$, but the mean of the Row 7 distribution is an order of magnitude larger than the mean of the Row 8 distribution. Probability of convergence to equality is (at least very close to) one for the Row 8 distribution.

This chapter's appendix reproduces the *Mathematica* simulation program.

E. SIMULATIONS OF THE DYNAMICS OF $B(h^*)$ FOR A CONTINUOUS DISTRIBUTION

We simulated the dynamic sequence for continuous distributions as well. Here we present results taking the initial distribution to be the log-normal with mean 40 and median 30. We vary the choice of h^*. For any lognormal distribution, with median m, we have $\int \log h \, dF(h) = \log m$. Hence, if we choose $h^* = m$ then, in the normalized distribution, we have $\rho(F^0) = 0$, and convergence of human capital to equality will occur with probability zero. In other words, we must choose $h^* < m$ to have a positive probability of convergence.

We chose a pair (h^*, p) where p is the probability of a Left victory, constant across time. We simulate an election. If the winning policy at date t is X, then we define the distribution of human capital at the next date by

$$F^{t+1}(S(h)) = F^t(h);$$

in other words, F^{t+1} is the mapping that associates $h^b\left(\frac{X(h)}{X(1)}\right)^{1-b}$ with $F^t(h)$, for all non-negative h. Rather than compute this mapping analytically, we approximated it by a graph of 50,000 points. The function so determined can be integrated numerically, and hence we can compute the Right and Left policies at the next date. We simulated each sequence for eighty generations (one *history*), and we declare convergence to equality to have occurred if the square of the coefficient of variation becomes less than 10^{-5}. If convergence occurs, it usually does so long before eighty generations.

To estimate the probability of convergence with a given choice (h^*, p), we simulated a collection of 100 histories, and computed the fraction of those that converged to equality. We present the results

Table 4.2. *Simulations of the sequence B(h*), b = 0.5.*

Collection #	h^*	p	$\rho(F^0)$	prob. of convergence
1	25	.405	.182	26%
2	25	.303	.182	8%
3	29	.482	.034	4%
4	20	.296	.405	32%
5	5	.405	1.79	100%

in Tables 4.2 and 4.3, where the five collections of histories reported have the same initial conditions *except* the value of b which is 0.5 for Table 4.2 and 0.6 for Table 4.3.

There are no surprises in these tables. Holding constant p, the probability of convergence to equality increases as h^* becomes smaller because that means the normalized distribution is more skewed (compare runs 1 and 5). Holding the pivot constant, and lowering the probability of Left victory (p), lowers the probability of convergence (compare runs 1 and 2). If h^* is very close to the median, so $\rho(F^0)$ is close to zero, then the probability of convergence is small, even if p is relatively large (run 3). Finally, increasing the value of b decreases the probability of convergence: a large value of b means that the effect of education is relatively less important in determining wages. (With $b = 1$, the distribution of human capital would never change.)

I am most grateful to Cong Huang for programming these simulations, which required writing an accurate and fast routine for numerical integration. (For this job, *Mathematica* was hopelessly slow and

Table 4.3. *Simulations of the sequence B(h*), b = 0.6.*

Collection #	h^*	p	$\rho(F^0)$	prob. of convergence
1	25	.405	.182	15%
2	25	.303	.182	5%
3	29	.482	.034	3%
4	20	.296	.405	26%
5	5	.405	1.79	100%

inaccurate.) For those who wish to carry out their own simulations, the program is available on my website, *http://pantheon.yale.edu/~jer39/*.

F. CONCLUSION

Here are the results of this chapter.

1. In a model with a unidimensional affine policy space, and median-voter (Hotelling-Downs) politics, the dynamic process converges to equality of human capital if and only if the initial distribution is strongly skewed, that is, when

$$\int \log h \, dF(h) \geq \log m$$

where m is the median of F.

    We next consider quasi-PUNEs in the infinite-dimensional policy space where the pivot dynasty remains fixed over time. We assume $b + c = 1$, in order to focus upon the role of political competition, instead of the role of technology, in determining convergence to equality.

2. In any stochastic dynamic sequence $A(h^*)$, when the equilibria lie on the upper envelope of the equilibrium manifold, the CVHC decreases monotonically to a positive number. Opportunist politics *never* engender equality of human capital in the long run.

3. In any stochastic dynamic sequence $B(h^*)$, when the equilibria lie on the lower envelope of the manifold, then with probability one, the CVHC converges to zero if and only if $\rho(F^t) \geq 0$ at all dates t. (The stated condition is characterizing of convergence in the almost sure case that Left wins an infinite number of times.)

4. From simulations of the process $B(h^*)$ for discrete initial distributions with three mass points, we conjecture that convergence to equality occurs with positive probability if $\rho(F^0)$ and $F^0(h^*)$ are sufficiently large. Indeed, if these two numbers

are sufficiently large, then we conjecture that convergence to equality occurs with probability close to one.

5. Our conjecture about convergence to equality of human capital for sequences $B(h^*)$ is confirmed by simulating the process for a lognormal distribution. The higher the probability of Left victory at each date and the smaller the pivot dynasty, the larger is the probability of convergence to equality.

6. The precise characterization of the probability of convergence on the lower envelope of the quasi-PUNE manifold is an open question.

It is interesting to note that the Downsian result does not provide a particularly good indicator of what happens when we work on the infinite-dimensional policy space. Why do we get convergence to equality, in the Downsian case, when the initial distribution is strongly skewed, but never, with opportunist politics, in the infinite-dimensional case? The reason is that, on the unidimensional policy space, the ideal policy for the median voter (when his wage is less than the mean) is *also* the ideal policy of the poorest voters. But on the infinite-dimensional space, the ideal policy of the pivot voter (who could be the median voter) is *never* the ideal policy for the poor. This indicates the importance of working with a model of *ruthless competition*. The unidimensional model is, at least *a priori*, artificially restrictive.

Both Downsian and PUNE politics, however, share this feature: convergence to equality only occurs if the initial distribution is strongly skewed – or, in the PUNE case, when $\rho(F^0) > \log h^*$. In other words, the pivot voter (or the median voter) must be relatively poor. What is the intuition behind this fact? Perhaps if the pivot voter is relatively rich, that is, $\rho(F^0) < \log h^*$, then the Right party represents only (relatively rich) citizens. Its equilibrium policies are (relatively) regressive; competition forces the Left party to also be relatively regressive, to maintain the allegiance of the pivot.

It is perhaps worthwhile remarking that, in real nations, more equal income distributions (in the sense of a smaller coefficient of variation) are *less* skewed than more unequal ones. (This fact was emphasized in the discussion that followed the publication of Persson and Tabellini [1994].) I believe that a major explanation for this difference between reality and the model is the role of altruism, or solidarity, among citizens. More equal income distributions are, I believe, often the result of more solidarism. Our utility function has presumed that each voter is interested only in his or her own dynasty, and so that solidarity remains unmodeled here.

APPENDIX, *MATHEMATICA* PROGRAM

Dynamic Simulations for a three-point distribution. This seems to provide convincing evidence that convergence occurs with positive prob in the B(h*) sequence.

```
Date[ ]
{2004, 12, 2, 18, 34, 49.328015}
```

The solutions labelled XL and XR hold when Right must compromise; YL and YR hold when Left must compromise. Refer to the above chapter for definitions of the following:

$$yls := \frac{h2\,(1-m3)+m1\,m3\,h3}{m2+m1\,m3}$$

$$y1 := Min[yls,\ h3]$$

$$x1 := m3\,(h3-y1)$$

$$x2 := \mu-1$$

$$y2 := which\left[m3\,h2<1-(m1\,h1+m2\,h2),\right.$$

$$\frac{1-m1\,h1-m2\,h2}{m3}\,,\ True\,,\ \frac{1-m1\,h1}{1-m1}\left.\right]$$

$$\mu := m1\,h1+m2\,h2+m3\,h3$$

$$Q[y\_] := m1\,h1+m2\,h2+m3\,y$$

$$y3s := \frac{\mu-x1-1+m1}{m1}$$

$$y3h := y3s-h1$$

$$S[h\_,X\_] := h^b\left(\frac{x[h]}{x[1]}\right)^{1-b}$$

σ := Which [Q[y1] $\geq$ 1, 1, True, 0]

σ := Which [ran $\leq$ m1, 1, True, 0]

r := m1 Log[h1]+m2Log[h2]+m3Log[h3]

y3 := Which [Q[y1] $\leq$ 1, y3s, True, y3h]

x3 := x1+y3

XL[h_] := μ

YR[h_] := x1+Min[h, y1]

XR[h_] := x2+Min[h, y2]

YL[h_] := Max[x3, x1+Min[h, 1]]

X[h_] := δ(σXL [h]+(1-σ) YL [h])+(1-δ) (σXR[h]

+ (1-σ) YR[h])

cvhc := $\dfrac{\text{Sqrt} [\text{m1} (\text{h1}-\mu)^2 + \text{m2} (\text{h2}-\mu)^2 + \text{m3} (\text{h3}-\mu)^2]}{\mu}$

The function 'lower' gives the lower bound of values of h3, which renders $r > 0$.

lower := $\text{Exp}\left[\dfrac{-\text{m2Log[h2]}-\text{m1Log[h1]}}{\text{m3}}\right]$

- **The program 'computerB' runs a simulation of fifty generations, declaring convergence to E has occurred if $h1(t) > 1 - 10^{-7}$. The program exits with a value of NN, which is one if convergence occurred and zero otherwise.**

```
computerB := (Do [NN=1; ran=Random[ ];
{h1n, h2n, h3n}=(S[h1, X], S[h2,X],S[h3, X];
{h1, h2, h3}={h1n, h2n, h3n};
If [μ<1, NN=0; Goto[outer]];
If [h1 ≥ 1.-10⁻⁷, Goto[outer]], {i,50}]; Label[outer])
General :: spelli :
Possible spelling error: new symbol name "outer"
is similar to existing symbol "outer." More...
{m1, m2, m3} = {.5, .3, .2}; b = .5;
```

- **Now we do long runs and look at the convergence properties.**

- **This run is with {m1, m2, m3}-=**

```
{m1, m2, m3}
{0.5, 0.3, 0.2};
```

- **The next command runs 500 super-iterations of computerB, and counts the fraction of such collections of histories in which convergence to E occurs. It carries this out ten times.**

```
Do[ JJ = 500;  count = 0;
   Do[{ h1,  h2,  h3} = {.5,  1.3,  20.}; computerB;
   count = count +  NN, { j,  jj}];
   Print["fraction converge= ",  N[ count/JJ ]], { kk, 10}]
```

```
fraction converge= 0.168
fraction converge= 0.18
fraction converge= 0.174
fraction converge= 0.168
fraction converge= 0.128
fraction converge= 0.164
fraction converge= 0.136
fraction converge= 0.162
fraction converge= 0.172
fraction converge= 0.138
```

- **The next command computes one collection of 5,000 histories, each fifty generations long. Presumably, the fraction of histories that converge here is a good estimate of the probability of convergence.**

```
Do[ JJ= 5000;  count= 0;
   Do[{h1, h2, h3}={.5, 1.3, 20.}; computerB;
   count= count+NN, {j, JJ}];
   Print["fraction converge= ",  N[ count/JJ ]], {kk, 1}]
```

```
fraction converge= 0.1646
```

$$\{m1,m2,m3\}=\{.6,.2,.2\}; \quad \text{Do}[\ JJ=5000; \quad \text{count}=0;$$

$$\text{Do}[\{h1,h2,h3\}=\{.5,1.3,7.\}; \quad \text{computerB};$$

$$\text{count}= \text{count}+NN,\{j,\ JJ\}];$$

$$\text{Print}\left["\text{fraction converge}=",\ N\left[\frac{\text{count}}{JJ}\right]\right],\{kk,1\}\right]$$

```
fraction converge= 0.0322
```

$$\{m1,m2,m3\} = \{.3,.5,.2\}; \quad \text{Do}[\ JJ=5000; \quad \text{count}=0;$$

$$\text{Do}[\{h1,h2,h3\} = \{.5,1.3,7.\}; \quad \text{computerB};$$

$$\text{count}= \text{count}+NN,\{j,\ JJ\}];$$

$$\text{Print}\left["\text{fraction converge}=",\ N\left[\frac{\text{count}}{JJ}\right]\right];\{kk,1\}]$$

```
fraction converge= 0.0012
```

$$\{m1,m2,m3\}=\{.8,.1,.1\}; \quad \text{Do}[\ JJ=5000; \quad \text{count}=0;$$

$$\text{Do}[\{h1,h2,h3\}=\{.5,1.3,200.\}; \quad \text{computerB};$$

$$\text{count}= \text{count}+ NN,\{j,\ JJ\}];$$

$$\text{Print}\left["\text{fraction converge}=",\ N\left[\frac{\text{count}}{JJ}\right]\right],\{kk,1\}]$$

```
fraction converge= 0.077
```

$$\{m1,m2,m3\} = \{.5,.3,.2\}; \quad \text{Do}[\ JJ=5000; \quad \text{count}=0;$$

$$\text{Do}[\{h1,h2,h3\}=\{.5,1.3,10^4\}; \quad \text{computerB};$$

$$\text{count}= \text{count}+NN,\{j,\ JJ\}];$$

$$\text{Print}\left["\text{fraction converge}=",\ N\left[\frac{\text{count}}{JJ}\right]\right];\{kk,1\}]$$

$$\text{Do}[JJ=5000; \quad \text{count}=0; \quad \text{Do}[\{h1,h2,h3\}=\{.5,1.3,10^6\};$$

$$\text{computerB};$$

$$\text{count}= \text{count}+NN,\{j,\ JJ\}];$$

$$\text{print}["\text{fraction converge}=",\ N\left[\frac{\text{count}}{JJ}\right]],\{\ kk,1\}]$$

```
fraction converge= 0.5524
fraction converge = 0.6722
```

$$\text{Do}[JJ=5000; \quad \text{count}=0;$$

$$\text{Do}[\{h1,h2,h3\}=\{.5,1.3,10^9\}; \quad \text{computerB};$$

$$\text{count}= \text{count}+NN,\{j,\ JJ\}];$$

```
Print["fraction converge= ",  N[count/JJ]] ; {kk, 1}]
```

fraction converge= 0.7574

```
Do[JJ= 5000;  count= 0;
   Do[{h1, h2, h3}= {.9, 4., 10^9}; computerB;
   count= count+ NN, {j,  JJ}];
   Print["fraction converge= ",  N[count/JJ]] ; {kk, 1}]
```

fraction converge= 0.9672

CHAPTER 5

The Dynamics of Human Capital with Endogenous Growth

A. THE EDUCATIONAL PRODUCTION FUNCTION WITH ENDOGENOUS GROWTH

In the analysis of Chapters 3 and 4, exogenous growth is permitted, in the sense that we can assume that the educational technology at date t is defined by

$$h' = \alpha^t h^b r^c,$$

where t is a time superscript, and the sequence $\{\alpha^t\}$ is exogenously given.[1] Exogenous technical change means that the value of α^t is independent of political decisions. Because we have not included capital in the wage function, we must assume that the influence of capital on marginal productivity, and hence on the wage, is captured in α^t. Thus, investment must be uninfluenced by political decisions. This is unrealistic, but perhaps no more unrealistic than the assumption that labor is inelastically supplied in our model: investment is also inelastically supplied.

Because we are concentrating on the role of education, however, it is inappropriate to ignore the effects of education on the technology, and so we should recognize the possibility of growth that is endogenous in our model, in the sense of the production function's being influenced by decisions on educational policy. Thus, we now consider a modified

---

[1] We can see this immediately, by noting that, in all the dynamic calculations, we take ratios of wages of pairs of dynasties, and the α term drops out.

educational technology given by

$$h' = \alpha^t h^b r^c \bar{r}^d, \tag{5.1}$$

where $\bar{r}$ is the average educational investment in generation t's children. We may think of $\bar{r}$ as influencing the quality of the technology, either in the sense that a higher level of education produces better research and development, or because a more educated work force is capable of using a more sophisticated technology, which is therefore built, or both.

I noted earlier that in our first model, the social and private returns to education were identical. This is no longer the case with the technology of Equation (5.1). Thus, society may have an interest in investing more in your child than you wish to invest because of the external effects your child, among many others, will have on aggregate productivity.

Thus, we can no longer expect that parties will propose to disaggregate the total resource bundle into consumption and investment exactly as each family would like. One consequence is that we will no longer be able to simplify the analysis by looking at the reduced policy space T^*: we shall have to work on the policy space T, which preserves the distinction between the consumption and investment policies.

B. INTUITION ON DYNAMICS

Let us first note that, under a laissez-faire policy, as before, the distribution of human capital is unchanged from one generation to the next, except for a multiplicative constant. If parents decide privately on educational investment, then each appropriately assumes aggregate investment is fixed and unchangeable by his or her action, and so an h parent invests $\frac{\gamma c}{1+\gamma c} h$ in his or her child's education, and consequently

$$h' = \alpha h^b \left(\frac{\gamma c}{1 + \gamma c} \right)^c h^c \bar{r}^d,$$

whence the ratio of human capitals of the sons of h_1 and h_2 is:

$$\left(\frac{h_1'}{h_2'} \right) = \left(\frac{h_1}{h_2} \right)^{b+c},$$

just as in the first model. So under laissez-faire the CVHC converges to zero, stays constant, or explodes, as returns to private investment are decreasing, constant, or increasing, respectively. It is therefore again appropriate for us to study the constant-returns case in this model because of the clean separation it provides between the roles of politics and technology.

Suppose c were close to zero, but d were significantly positive. Then there would be small private returns to education, but significant social returns. Political parties, which represent large coalitions, would be interested in making educational investments. Individual parents would also want society to invest in education, but they would want almost all of *their* family's total resource bundle devoted to consumption. Indeed, in this case, we might conjecture that society would invest approximately equally in all children. In this case, if $b < 1$, then wages would tend to equality because the ratio of the human capitals in any two dynasties would approach one. Such policies, we conjecture, would be Pareto efficient, in the policy space, and hence both parties would advocate policies of this form.

So we can surmise that, in the case $c > 0$ and $d > 0$, there will be more of a tendency toward equality of wages than in the case where returns to investment are only private. We will therefore concentrate on the case of equilibria in sequence $A(h^*)$, where politics are dominated by opportunism. Will we achieve equality of wages in the long run, even with opportunistic politics, if $d > 0$? If so, then our previous work strongly suggests that any sequence of equilibria with 'invariant pivot' will bring about equality of wages.

C. QUASI-PUNEs ON THE UPPER ENVELOPE
OF THE EQUILIBRIUM MANIFOLD

As I remarked, the problem of characterizing quasi-PUNEs with the endogenous-growth technology is more difficult than the first one we studied because we no longer can work on the reduced policy space where parties are choosing only the total-resource-bundle function. We must return to policy space T with elements (ψ, r). (See Chapter 3, page 42.) We will indeed work on a subset of T, namely the set of policies

$$\hat{T} = \{(\psi, r) \in T \mid 0 \leq \psi' \leq 1, \ 0 \leq r' \leq 1\}.$$

Thus, we now require that the consumption and investment functions *each* be non-decreasing.

The analogs of Propositions 3.3 and 3.4 continue to hold in this environment, and so there is, again, a manifold of quasi-PUNEs, whose lower boundary comprises those equilibria where the Militants in each party are powerful, and whose upper boundary comprises those equilibria where the Opportunists are powerful. On the upper boundary, both parties propose the ideal policy of the pivot type, h^*. We are interested in whether dynamic sequences of quasi-PUNEs on this envelope converge to equality of human capital.

We have two theorems that characterize the PUNEs in the sequence $A(h^*)$, depending on the size of h^*.

Let $\mathbf{F}$ be the probability measure of human capital at a given date. Recall the definition of the function

$$Q(h) = \int_0^h x d\mathbf{F}(x) + h(1 - F(h)).$$

Theorem 5.1. *Let (ψ^*, r^*) be the policy at a quasi-PUNE on the upper boundary of the manifold of quasi-PUNEs at the pivot h^*, when the CDF is F. Suppose that:*

$$(A1) \ \frac{d}{c} \leq \frac{\mu - Q(h^*)}{\gamma c h^*} - 1, \ and$$

$$(A2) \ \frac{d}{c} \geq \frac{1 - F(h^*)}{F(h^*)}.$$

Then the investment in all types is a constant given by:

$$r^*(h) \equiv \bar{r} = \gamma(c + d)y,$$

where $\ y = \dfrac{\mu + h^* - Q(h^*)}{1 + \gamma(c + d)}.$

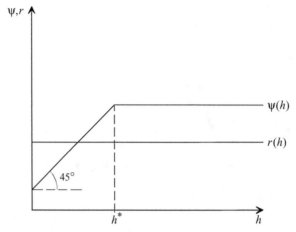

Figure 5.1(a). Policies of Theorem 5.1.

Consumption is given by:

$$\psi^*(h) = \begin{cases} h - h^* + y, & \text{if } h \le h^* \\ y, & \text{if } h > h^* \end{cases}.$$

Proof: See Appendix.   ∎

The policy is illustrated in Figure 5.1(a). The assumptions (A1) and (A2) place upper and lower bounds on the relative size of the external and internal elasticities, d/c. For example, if we take the pivot h^* to be the median, then we must have $d > c$ (according to (A2)), while (A1) tells us that γ must be sufficiently small. These are both intuitive statements: if $d > c$ then a parent cares about total investment in education, while if γ is small, he or she is relatively unconcerned with investment in his or her child. Thus, in this case, it is not unsurprising that the equilibrium policy entails equal investment in all children.

If we begin in the sequence $A(h^*)$, with an economy in which (A2) and (A1) hold, then (A2) holds forever. If (A1) held forever, we would surely converge to equality of wages, if $b < 1$, because the same amount is being invested in all children. Unfortunately, we will observe that the r.h.s. of (A1) eventually becomes negative, and so the inequality ceases to hold; so eventually we leave the regime of Theorem 5.1.

We therefore require an analysis of what occurs in the sequence $A(h^*)$ when (A1) no longer holds. We have:

Theorem 5.2. *Suppose that:*

$$(B1) \frac{d}{c} > \frac{\mu - Q(h^*)}{\gamma ch^*} - 1, \ and$$

$$(B2) \frac{d}{c} \geq \frac{r_0 + Q(h_1)}{r_0 + h_1} \frac{1 - F(h^*)}{F(h^*) - F(h_1)},$$

where (r_0, h_1) is the solution of the system of equations:

$$(B3a)\, r_0 = \mu - Q(h^*),$$

$$(B3b) \frac{1}{h^* - h_1} = \frac{\gamma c}{r_0 + h_1} + \frac{\gamma d}{r_0 + Q(h_1)}(1 - F(h_1)).$$

Then the quasi-PUNE at h^* on the upper boundary of the quasi-PUNE manifold has both parties proposing the policy (r^*, ψ^*) given by:

$$r^*(h) = \begin{cases} r_0 + h, & for\ 0 \leq h \leq h_1 \\ r_0 + h_1, & for\ h > h_1 \end{cases}$$

and

$$\psi^*(h) = \begin{cases} 0, & for\ h \leq h_1 \\ h - h_1, & for\ h_1 < h \leq h^* \\ h^* - h_1, & for\ h > h^*. \end{cases}$$

We have $h_1 < h^*$.

Proof: See Appendix. ∎

The policy is illustrated in Figure 5.1(b). This theorem's premises say that the ratio d/c must be sufficiently large. If it is, then the educational policy will entail constant investment in all children who come from families with human capital larger than h_1. The critical question, with regard to convergence to equality of human capital, will be how small h_1 becomes in the dynamic process.

From Figures 5.1(a) and (b), we note that in the policies of both Theorems 5.1 and 5.2, the total resource bundle has the same shape as it did in h^*'s ideal policy in the model with exogenous technical

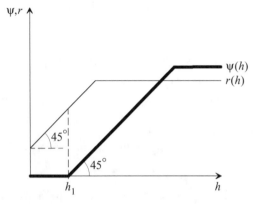

Figure 5.1(b).

change. The ideal, for h^*, is to hold all types who are richer than he or she to his or her total resources, and to decrease total resources as rapidly as possible for those who are less rich than he or she. However, the partition of total resources into consumption and investment is very different from before. If h^* is sufficiently small (viz., assumption (A1)) then the partition of total resources between consumption and investment at h^* is the individually optimal partition for h^*. (Note that, in the policy of Theorem 5.1, $r^*(h^*) = \gamma(c + d)\psi^*(h^*)$.) However, for h^* large (in the sense of (B1)), decreasing total resources from their optimal value at h^*, at a rate of unity, and keeping educational investment sufficiently high, requires allocating zero consumption to the very poor types. At this policy, it is not hard to verify that $r^*(h) > \gamma(c + d)\psi(h)$ for all h. Thus, keeping investment high requires even h^* to misallocate his or her total resources, from the individual viewpoint.

D. DYNAMICS

We see that in the regime of Theorem 5.2, investment is constant for $h > h_1$. Since at every date, $h_1^t < h^{*t}$, it follows that the ratio of wages of any two dynasties with initial human capital larger than h^* tends to one, if $b < 1$. The question that we must answer to completely understand the dynamics of human capital in these quasi-PUNEs is, what happens to the value h_1^t? We have:

Theorem 5.3. *Let $b + c = 1$. Suppose that for all $t = 0, 1, 2, \ldots$ the time-dated versions of conditions (B1) and (B2) of Theorem 5.2 hold where (r_0^t, h_1^t) is the time-dated solution of equations (B3a) and (B3b). Then:*

(1) $\lim F^t(h_1^t) = 0$,
(2) *the* CVHC *approaches zero in the dynamic process,*
(3) $\lim h_1^t = \dfrac{\gamma(c+d)}{1 + \gamma(c+d)} \lim h^{*t}$, *and*
(4) *condition (B2) approaches condition (A2) [of Theorem 5.1].*

Proof: See Appendix. ∎

Because of conclusion (1), it follows that, for large t, the same is invested in virtually all children, and hence wages tend to equality. To be precise, given any two original Eves with non-zero human capital, there exists a date T, such that, for all $t > T$, the same amount is invested in the education of the descendents in these dynasties, and hence the ratio of their human capitals tends to one. Thus conclusion (2) follows immediately from (1).

We may therefore conclude that if the ratio d/c is sufficiently large, then wages converge to equality, even with opportunist politics. 'Sufficiently large' means, in the case where (A1) holds, that (A2) is true, and in the case where (B1) holds, that (B2) is true.

Because of (4), it follows that condition (A2) is *essentially* what is needed concerning the ratio d/c. In particular, if h^* is the median of the distribution, then we require $d > c$.

I next provide a simulation. I begin with the lognormal distribution with mean 40 and median 30, and choose h^* to be the median. It is convenient to normalize by setting the median equal to unity at all dates: this does not affect the coefficients of variation. I choose $\gamma = 0.75$, $b = c = 0.5$, $d = 0.6$. The critical ratio is $d/c = 1.2$. At date 0, we are in the regime of Theorem 5.2: both (B1) and (B2) hold. Table 5.1 presents the results of a three-generation simulation: The

Table 5.1.

Data	h1	F'[h1]	Ratio
0	0.157662	0.00743808	1.01475
1	0.344178	0.00300324	1.00582
2	0.405122	0.0000628779	1.00012

last column presents the ratio at the r.h.s. of condition (B2) at each date; we require that this ratio be less than or equal to 1.2. We see that the convergence claimed in conclusion (1) of Theorem 5.3 appears to be occurring rapidly: by date 2, the same amount is being invested in virtually all children – that is, in over 99.99 percent of all children. From conclusion (3) of Theorem 5.3, we know that h_1^t is converging to approximately 0.452.

Another glimpse of the speed of convergence is provided by looking at the CDFs of human capital in dates 0 and 2 of the above simulation. They are provided in Figure 5.2. The medians have been normalized to one in these graphs.

We see the convergence to equality appears to be rapid. And recall, this is in the PUNE where politics are most opportunistic, which is when the convergence to equality is least rapid, in the manifold of quasi-PUNEs.

E. WHY PUBLIC EDUCATION?

It is interesting to observe what the ratio $r(h)/\psi(h)$ looks like in these solutions. I noted earlier that $r(h)/\psi(h) > \gamma c$ for all h in the solution of Theorem 5.2. This means that every type would like to redistribute the total resource bundle assigned to its family toward consumption and away from educational investment. This desire will be strongest among the poorest types. We thus see, in this model, an important role for public financing of education: assuming the usual free-rider psychology, it would not be possible to realize these solutions with private financing of education. Political parties here overcome the free-rider

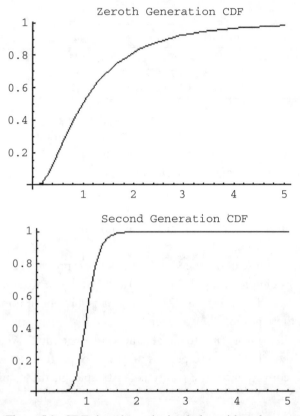

Figure 5.2. CDFs in a dynamic simulation with endogenous growth.

problem because they represent large coalitions of citizens. Parties in quasi-PUNEs always propose Pareto efficient solutions, subject to the constraints on policy.

Indeed, we note that, in this 'opportunist' solution, after-tax income is zero for a poor section of the population. This is to be interpreted as consumption being driven down to subsistence level.

It might not be empirically correct that *every* type – even the rich – would like to shift the resources dedicated to its family away from education toward consumption. Many of the wealthy send their children to public universities, but pay as tuition only a small fraction of true costs, and for these families, we cannot reject the claim that the family would prefer to reallocate some (public) education funds to private consumption. If the child attends a private university, however, the wealthy family will pay a substantial fraction of the true costs as tuition, and for these families, we cannot argue that too much, from the private viewpoint, is being invested in the child's education. At many private universities in the United States today, students are admitted independently of their parents' ability to pay; when such a student is admitted, the university finances a large part of educational costs out of other (endowment) income. It is consistent with observation to hold that these families would prefer to reallocate some funds spent on their child's education to consumption. And why are relatively poor families willing to pay taxes to support public universities? Because (according to our model) of the positive externality the education thus provided bestows on *their* children, who may not attend the university, but whose wages will benefit from the education of the more privileged or talented.

Thus, to repeat this important point, it is consistent to say that, at the policy recommended by a party, given the total resources devoted to his or her family (after-tax income plus educational investment), almost all (or at least a very large fraction of) parents would rather redistribute toward consumption and away from investment, *and* that given the constraints on policy, the solutions are Pareto efficient.

What happens if the ratio d/c is not as large as the conditions in Theorems 5.1 and 5.2 require? We know that if $d = 0$, we definitely do not get convergence to wage equality – that was our first model in the equilibria on the paths $A(h^*)$. Doubtless, when d/c becomes sufficiently small, but still positive, convergence to equality no longer occurs with opportunist politics.

F. CONCLUSION

Let me sum up the analysis thus far. We began by analyzing the model where returns to education are completely private. We showed that, if politics are ideological, then in a sequence of quasi-PUNEs where the probability of each party's victory remains constant over time, convergence to equality of human capital occurs with positive probability (by that convergence we mean that the ratio of the levels of human capital in any two dynasties approaches unity over time) only if the original distribution of human capital is strongly showed. If politics are very opportunistic, then convergence to equality of human capital never occurs.

In contrast, we showed that in a unidimensional model, with opportunist politics (the Hotelling-Downs model), convergence to equality of wages occurs if and only if the initial distribution of human capital is strongly and positively skewed. That result shows the value of working on a large policy space. Large policy spaces are the reality, and it makes a difference to model politics thusly.

We then considered an educational technology with endogenous growth, one in which the general level of educational investment has a positive effect on all wages. One interpretation is that the sophistication of machines and technology is positively related to the level of education, and hence, so is labor productivity and hence wages. We showed that if the ratio d/c is sufficiently large, then, over time, even in the quasi-PUNEs with opportunist politics, we tend to a state in which the same amount is invested in all children, which induces equality of levels of human capital.

All these statements are true for the constant-returns case, when $b + c = 1$, a case that allows us to separate the role of technology from the role of democracy. If decreasing returns are the reality, then we presume that our theorems transform into statements about the relative speed of convergence to equality of wages.

CHAPTER 6

Estimation of Technological Parameters

The values of the elasticities in the production function

$$h' = \alpha h^b r^c \bar{r}^d$$

have been of key importance in the analysis. In this chapter, I present results of attempts to estimate the coefficients b, c, and d for the United States, by estimating the linear relation

$$\log h' = \log \alpha + b \log h + c \log r + d \log \bar{r}. \tag{6.1}$$

Using the National Longitudinal Study of Youth (NLSY 2000), we observed the income of young men in their mid-thirties in 2000 (h'). By using a previous year of the NLSY, we observed the income of the individual's family in 1979 (h). To compute r, the amount invested in the education of the individual, we summed two quantities: the estimated secondary school educational investment and the post-secondary investment. We took the first of these quantities to be the per-capita expenditures on public schools of the SMSA (standard metropolitan statistical area) in which the individual resided in 2000 (thus assuming he attended school in the same city); we estimated the second quantity as the per-capita expenditures of the college the individual attended on instruction, multiplying by the number of years of post-secondary education the individual received.

Estimating the average educational investment in the cohort of the individual was trickier. In our model, the cohort with whom an individual attends school is also the cohort with whom he works. Thus, we estimated $\bar{r}$ as the average educational investment in the population of workers in the SMSA in which the individual works. We computed this as follows. First, from the census, we constructed the joint distribution of (age, years of education) of the labor force in each SMSA. Then, using the Digest of Educational Statistics, we computed the state educational expenditures per capita in 1990, 1980, 1970, and 1960, and the national expenditure per capita in 1955. Using these data, we computed from the above estimated joint distribution the average educational investment in the labor force of each SMSA. This is our estimate of $\bar{r}$.

We then performed the regression (6.1), including a variety of other demographic variables as independent variables.

The details of the data analysis are described in the Appendix to this chapter.

In Tables 6.1, 6.2, and 6.3 we present three OLS regressions, with different versions of the variable $\log h'$. The coefficients b, c, and d are labeled 'log fam inc,' 'log educ exp,' and 'log avg educ,' respectively – the third, fourth, and fifth variables in these regressions.

The values for b and c are highly statistically significant: b ranges 0.205 to 0.217 in the three regressions, and c ranges from 0.086 to 0.104. Thus $b > c$, and $b + c$ is significantly less than unity. The estimates of d, however, are not at all precise. Although in two of the regressions, the estimated value of d is negative, no importance should be attached to this fact because the estimates are not statistically significant. Our data do not permit us to estimate d. They do not permit us to say that d is zero.

We observe that all the other variables, when significant, enter with the expected signs.

We also performed quantile regressions using the same three dependent variables because we thought that perhaps the coefficients in (6.1) were sensitive to the quantile of the distribution of wages. These results were essentially the same as the ones just reported; b and c are precisely estimated, but not d. The results of these regressions are presented in the data appendix.

We note that, even had our regressions generated precise estimates of d, they probably would underestimate the value of d that is appropriate for our theory. The value d from these regressions would be the elasticity of wages with respect to human capital in a cross-section

Table 6.1. *OLS regression of equation (6.1), dependent variable logarithm of three-year smoothed average of wage and salary income.*

Multiple Imputation Estimates

Model: regress

Dependent Variable: log_avg_ws

Number of Observations: 6403

	Coef.	Std. Err.	t	Df	P>|t|
son_age	.00348	.0061305	0.567	82	0.572
dad_age	.0002	.0020095	0.101	21	0.920
log_fam_inc	.20477	.0367649	5.570	47	0.000
log_educ_exp	.10409	.0104118	9.997	9	0.000
log_avg_educ	−.06128	.2177555	−0.281	11	0.784
south	−.05537	.0373411	−1.483	13	0.162
foreign_lang	−.05392	.0493022	−1.094	35	0.282
sibs	−.01492	.0087085	−1.714	8	0.127
military	.19275	.0704956	2.734	8	0.025
outside_home	−.15839	.0667266	−2.374	9	0.041
urban	.05615	.0269317	2.085	119	0.039
married	.68642	.033345	20.585	50	0.000
separated	.2929	.0625341	4.684	72	0.000
divorced	.27915	.0512217	5.450	19	0.000
widowed	.71434	.2087587	3.422	33	0.002
live_dad_other_woman	−.03322	.0965019	−0.344	31	0.733
live_dad	−.22441	.144088	−1.557	13	0.144
live_mom_other_man	−.09269	.0511624	−1.812	41	0.077
live_mom	−.06299	.0404473	−1.557	27	0.131
live_other	−.10048	.068907	−1.458	40	0.153
black	−.23762	.041674	−5.702	28	0.000
asian	.09844	.1333406	0.738	35	0.465
native_am	−.0275	.0710981	−0.387	24	0.702
hispanic	−.09508	.0594812	−1.599	37	0.118
race_other	−.01665	.0372243	−0.447	387	0.655
protestant	.07301	.0623013	1.172	46	0.247
rom_cath	.12481	.0763329	1.635	17	0.120
jewish	.28775	.1854156	1.552	14	0.144
other_rel	.00898	.067916	0.132	96	0.895
_cons	8.3469	2.197159	3.799	11	0.003

Table 6.2. *OLS regression of equation (6.1), dependent variable logarithm of three-year smoothed average of wage, salary, real farm and business income.*

Multiple Imputation Estimates

Model: regress

Dependent Variable: log_avg_ws_fb

Number of Observations: 6403

	Coef.	Std. Err.	t	Df	P>|t|
son_age	.00272	.0064588	0.421	56	0.675
dad_age	.00109	.0021368	0.508	17	0.618
log_fam_inc	.21742	.0414079	5.251	23	0.000
log_educ_exp	.10077	.0103177	9.767	9	0.000
log_avg_educ	.00767	.2166893	0.035	12	0.972
south	−.07117	.0379132	−1.877	13	0.083
foreign_lang	−.05042	.0485583	−1.038	48	0.304
sibs	−.01694	.0088856	−1.907	8	0.095
military	.17394	.0775573	2.243	7	0.059
outside_home	−.14959	.0672122	−2.226	9	0.052
urban	.04779	.0284218	1.681	72	0.097
married	.68747	.0349267	19.683	40	0.000
separated	.27953	.0589993	4.738	367	0.000
divorced	.2714	.0531001	5.111	18	0.000
widowed	.7081	.2249568	3.148	24	0.004
live_dad_other_woman	−.06066	.1152068	−0.527	14	0.607
live_dad	−.23763	.1464479	−1.623	13	0.129
live_mom_other_man	−.08727	.0577845	−1.510	21	0.146
live_mom	−.06712	.042092	−1.595	24	0.124
live_other	−.06696	.0712614	−0.940	36	0.354
black	−.26482	.0436337	−6.069	24	0.000
asian	.07864	.1305736	0.602	52	0.550
native_am	−.04515	.0769163	−0.587	18	0.565
hispanic	−.10449	.0600292	−1.741	41	0.089
race_other	−.02689	.0378018	−0.711	486	0.477
protestant	.06733	.061876	1.088	62	0.281
rom_cath	.09452	.0754359	1.253	20	0.224
jewish	.26305	.1649866	1.594	25	0.123
other_rel	−.0027	.0703835	−0.038	78	0.970
_cons	7.6837	2.190249	3.508	12	0.004

Table 6.3. *OLS regression of Equation (6.1), logarithm of three-year smoothed average of average total net family income.*

Multiple Imputation Estimates

Model: regress

Dependent Variable: log_avg_net

Number of Observations: 6403

	Coef.	Std. Err.	t	Df	P>|t|
son_age	.0091	.0071576	1.271	14	0.225
dad_age	.00055	.0023038	0.240	9	0.816
log_fam_inc	.213	.0455654	4.675	10	0.001
log_educ_exp	.08588	.0057305	14.986	216	0.000
log_avg_educ	−.0211	.1316157	−0.160	231	0.873
south	−.0457	.0314971	−1.451	16	0.166
foreign_lang	−.03518	.0503869	−0.698	17	0.495
sibs	−.02243	.0084712	−2.648	7	0.034
military	.24478	.0623207	3.928	8	0.004
outside_home	−.12509	.0501957	−2.492	15	0.025
urban	.02081	.0241059	0.863	132	0.389
married	.8391	.0374072	22.432	14	0.000
separated	.2953	.0585347	5.045	46	0.000
divorced	.27661	.0573218	4.825	10	0.001
widowed	.19386	.2093602	0.926	18	0.367
live_dad_other_woman	−.04491	.0830435	−0.541	45	0.591
live_dad	−.11955	.1215061	−0.984	16	0.340
live_mom_other_man	−.04173	.0513081	−0.813	20	0.425
live_mom	−.00909	.0355091	−0.256	32	0.800
live_other	−.12919	.0608066	−2.125	48	0.039
black	−.21144	.0420704	−5.026	16	0.000
asian	−.01186	.1312326	−0.090	20	0.929
native_am	−.04702	.0705657	−0.666	15	0.515
hispanic	−.06965	.0547209	−1.273	32	0.212
race_other	−.02828	.0358591	−0.789	86	0.433
protestant	.12232	.1013989	1.206	7	0.270
rom_cath	.12971	.10136	1.280	7	0.242
jewish	.28944	.1570047	1.844	17	0.083
other_rel	.09806	.1072833	0.914	7	0.390
_cons	8.3669	1.328014	6.300	385	0.000

of SMSAs in the United States. But probably more significant than this effect is the nature of technological innovation that is adopted in a country, depending on the education and skill of its work force, and this effect we have not estimated. Clearly, cross-national regressions would be needed to estimate this; however, such regressions suffer from many other problems, not to mention the impossibility of collecting data for a panel of countries similar to that which we describe for the United States.

We therefore remain agnostic concerning the value of d; whether the ratio d/c is large enough to generate the convergence to equality in the distribution of human capital that the theorems in Chapter 5 describe is an open question.

DATA APPENDIX

The primary variables of interest include the amount of educational expenditure for each individual in the National Longitudinal Survey of Youth (NLSY 2000–2001). First, to ascertain the ages of R and R's father, we collected the following variables:

Variable Name	Variable Code
AGE OF R AT INTERVIEW DATE (2000)	R70075.00
YEAR OF BIRTH OF R's FATHER (1987)	R23031.00
AGE OF R's FATHER (1987)	R23032.00
YEAR OF BIRTH OF R's FATHER (1988)	R25053.00
AGE OF R's FATHER (1988)	R25054.00

From these variables we determined the age of the father and the son in 1979. Then, to establish a fixed reference age, we took the average father's age and the average son's age, and subtracted each from the actual age. This produced the following two variables:

Variable Name	Description
SON_AGE	The difference between R's age in 1979 and the average age of all R's in 1979
DAD_AGE	The difference between R's father's age in 1979 and the average age of all fathers' ages in 1979

Next, from the NLSY, we collected data on the income of the respondent (R)'s family in the survey year, 1979, as well as each respondent's income data, measured three ways, in 1996, 1998, and 2000.

Variable Name	Description	Variable Code
TOTAL NET FAMILY INCOME IN PAST CALENDAR YEAR (1979)	The total income of R's family in 1979	R01903.10
TOTAL INCOME FROM WAGES AND SALARY IN PAST CALENDAR YEAR (1996)	The total amount of wages and salary that R received in 1996	R56262.00
TOTAL INCOME FROM FARM OR BUSINESS IN PAST CALENDAR YEAR (1996)	The total amount that R earned from a farm or business in 1996	R56266.00
TOTAL NET FAMILY INCOME IN PAST CALENDAR YEAR (1996)	The total amount that R and his family earned in 1996	R51660.00
TOTAL INCOME FROM WAGES AND SALARY IN PAST CALENDAR YEAR (1998)	The total amount of wages and salary that R received in 1998	R63646.00
TOTAL INCOME FROM FARM OR BUSINESS IN PAST CALENDAR YEAR (1998)	The total amount that R earned from a farm or business in 1998	R63650.00
TOTAL NET FAMILY INCOME IN PAST CALENDAR YEAR (1998)	The total amount that R and his family earned in 1998	R64787.00
TOTAL INCOME FROM WAGES AND SALARY IN PAST CALENDAR YEAR (2000)	The total amount of wages and salary that R received in 2000	R69097.00
TOTAL INCOME FROM FARM OR BUSINESS IN PAST CALENDAR YEAR (2000)	The total amount that R earned from a farm or business in 2000	R69111.00
TOTAL NET FAMILY INCOME IN PAST CALENDAR YEAR (2000)	The total amount that R and his family earned in 2000	R70065.00

We divided each of these variables by the year's GDP deflator (1995 = 1) and took the natural logarithm of that answer to obtain the following variables:

Variable Name	Description
LOG_FAM	The natural logarithm of R's family's real income in 1979
LOG_WS_1996	The natural logarithm of R's real wages and salary in 1996
LOG_FB_1996	The natural logarithm of R's real farm and/or business income in 1996
LOG_TOT_FAM_1996	The natural logarithm of R's family's real total income in 1996
LOG_WS_1998	The natural logarithm of R's real wages and salary in 1998
LOG_FB_1998	The natural logarithm of R's real farm and/or business income in 1998
LOG_TOT_FAM_1998	The natural logarithm of R's family's real total income in 1998
LOG_WS_2000	The natural logarithm of R's real wages and salary in 2000
LOG_FB_2000	The natural logarithm of R's real farm and/or business income in 2000
LOG_TOT_FAM_2000	The natural logarithm of R's family's real total income in 2000

We also created several average variables that attempt to mitigate the effects of variations in income across years. These include the following:

Variable Name	Description
LOG_AVG_WS	The natural logarithm of the average of R's real wages and salary for the years 1996, 1998, and 2000
LOG_AVG_WS_FB	The natural logarithm of the average of the sum of R's real wages and salary and farm and/or business income for the years 1996, 1998, and 2000
LOG_AVG_NET	The natural logarithm of the average of R's family's real total income for the years 1996, 1998, and 2000

The other key variables also come from the NLSY, and include the educational expenditure on R and the average educational expenditure on each son in R's area of residence. We obtained these from the NLSY 2000 Geocode CD, Digest of Education Statistics from the US Department of Education, Integrated Public Use Microdata Series (IPUMS) archive at the University of Minnesota, and the National Science Foundation's WEBCAPSAR. The following data come from the NLSY 2000 Geocode CD:

Variable Name	Description	Variable Code
SMSA OF RESIDENCE (1979)		R02190.03
FICE CODE OF MOST RECENT COLLEGE ATTENDED (1984)		R15230.71
HIGHEST GRADE COMPLETED AS OF MAY 1 SURVEY YEAR (2000)	0 NONE	R70071.00
	93 PRE-KINDERGARTEN	
	94 KINDERGARTEN	
	1 1ST GRADE	
	2 2ND GRADE	
	3 3RD GRADE	
	4 4TH GRADE	
	5 5TH GRADE	
	6 6TH GRADE	
	7 7TH GRADE	
	8 8TH GRADE	
	9 9TH GRADE	
	10 10TH GRADE	
	11 11TH GRADE	
	12 12TH GRADE	
	13 1ST YEAR COLLEGE	
	14 2ND YEAR COLLEGE	
	15 3RD YEAR COLLEGE	
	16 4TH YEAR COLLEGE	
	17 5TH YEAR COLLEGE	
	18 6TH YEAR COLLEGE	
	19 7TH YEAR COLLEGE	
	20 8TH YEAR COLLEGE OR MORE	

The following data come from the Digest of Education Statistics:

Variable Name	Description
NATIONAL EDUCATIONAL EXPENDITURE (1955)	The average expenditure per student in average daily attendance in the United States in 1955
STATE EDUCATIONAL EXPENDITURE (1960)	The average expenditure per student in average daily attendance in each state in 1960
STATE EDUCATIONAL EXPENDITURE (1970)	The average expenditure per student in average daily attendance in each state in 1970
STATE EDUCATIONAL EXPENDITURE (1980)	The average expenditure per student in average daily attendance in each state in 1980
STATE EDUCATIONAL EXPENDITURE (1990)	The average expenditure per student in average daily attendance in each state in 1990

The following data come from the National Science Foundation:

Variable Name	Description
COMPUTED CURRENT EDUCATIONAL EXPENDITURES AND TRANSFERS PER INSTITUTION (1984)	The total amount of current educational expenditures and transfers per college or university in 1984
ENROLLMENT (1984)	The total enrollment per college or university in 1984

We used these data to create the following variables:

Variable Name	Description
LOG_TOT	The total amount of educational expenditure per student, defined as the real expenditure per state in the student's SMSA multiplied by his years of high school, plus real college educational expenditures divided by the number of students multiplied by his years of college

From the IPUMS, we obtained a 1 percent sample of the population of the United States with the following four characteristics:

Variable Name	Description	Variable Code
AGE	The age of the individual	AGE
MSA	The Metropolitan Statistical Area or Standard Metropolitan Statistical Area in which the individual lived	METAREA
EDUCATIONAL ATTAINMENT	Not applicable 00	EDUC99
	No school completed	01
	Nursery school	02
	Kindergarten	03
	1st-4th grade	04
	5th-8th grade	05
	9th grade	6
	10th grade	7
	11th grade	8
	12th grade, no diploma	9
	High school graduate, or GED	10
	Some college, no degree	11
	Associate degree, occupational program	12
	Associate degree, academic program	13
	Bachelor's degree	14
	Master's degree	15
	Professional degree	16
	Doctorate degree	17

From this, we created a joint distribution of age and educational attainment for each metropolitan area in the United States based on five age groups (21–31, 32–41, 42–51, 52–61, 62–65) and five educational attainment categories (less than high school, some high school, high school graduate, some college, and college graduate or more). We proceeded to create the following variable.

Variable Name	Description
LOG_SMSA	The average amount of educational investment per student in each SMSA, computed from the amount spent in the state of each SMSA in each respective year, multiplied by the percent of the SMSA labor force at that age and across educational levels, summed across education levels and ages

The control variables employed come from the NLSY (2000). These include the following:

Variable Name	Description	Variable Code
SOUTH-NONSOUTH RESIDENCE IN US AT AGE 14	1 if R was living in the South in 1979, 0 otherwise	R00016.10
WAS FOREIGN LANGUAGE SPOKEN AT HOME DURING R's CHILDHOOD?	1 if R's family spoke a language other than English at home, 0 otherwise	R00011.00
AREA OF RESIDENCE AT AGE 14 URBAN/RURAL?	1 if R lived in town or city, 2 if R lived in rural area, 3 if R lived on a farm	R00018.00
WITH WHOM DID R LIVE AT AGE 14?	11 FATHER-MOTHER 12 FATHER-STEPMOTHER 13 FATHER-OTHER WOMAN RELATIVE 14 FATHER-OTHER WOMAN 15 FATHER-NO WOMAN 19 FATHER-MISSING WOMAN 21 STEPFATHER-MOTHER 22 STEPFATHER-STEPMOTHER 23 STEPFATHER-WOMAN RELATIVE 24 STEPFATHER-OTHER WOMAN 25 STEPFATHER-NO WOMAN 31 MAN RELATIVE-MOTHER 32 MAN RELATIVE-STEPMOTHER 33 MAN RELATIVE-WOMAN RELATIVE 34 MAN RELATIVE-OTHER WOMAN 35 MAN RELATIVE-NO WOMAN 41 OTHER MAN-MOTHER 42 OTHER MAN-STEPMOTHER 43 OTHER MAN-WOMAN RELATIVE 44 OTHER MAN-OTHER WOMAN 45 OTHER MAN-NO WOMAN 51 NO MAN-MOTHER 52 NO MAN-STEPMOTHER 53 NO MAN-WOMAN RELATIVE 54 NO MAN-OTHER WOMAN 55 NO MAN-NO WOMAN	R00019.00

Variable Name	Description	Variable Code
	80 OTHER ARRANGEMENT	
	90 ON MY OWN	
	91 MISSING MAN-MOTHER	
	93 MISSING MAN-WOMAN	
	RELATIVE	
NUMBER OF SIBLINGS	The number of siblings that R has	R00091.00
1ST OR ONLY	0 NONE	R00096.00
RACIAL/ETHNIC	1 BLACK	
ORIGIN	2 CHINESE	
	3 ENGLISH	
	4 FILIPINO	
	5 FRENCH	
	6 GERMAN	
	7 GREEK	
	8 HAWAIIAN, P.I.	
	9 INDIAN-AMERICAN OR NATIVE	
	AMERICAN	
	10 ASIAN INDIAN	
	11 IRISH	
	12 ITALIAN	
	13 JAPANESE	
	14 KOREAN	
	15 CUBAN	
	16 CHICANO	
	17 MEXICAN	
	18 MEXICAN-AMER	
	19 PUERTO RICAN	
	20 OTHER HISPANIC	
	21 OTHER SPANISH	
	22 POLISH	
	23 PORTUGUESE	
	24 RUSSIAN	
	25 SCOTTISH	
	26 VIETNAMESE	
	27 WELSH	
	28 OTHER	
	29 AMERICAN	
RACIAL/ETHNIC ORIGIN WITH WHICH R IDENTIFIES MOST CLOSELY (> 1 ORIGIN)	R's primary racial/ethnic identification, if R has more than one (codes the same as above)	R00102.00
PRESENT RELIGIOUS	0 NONE, NO RELIGION	R00104.00

(*continued*)

Variable Name	Description	Variable Code
AFFILIATION 79 INT (COLLAPSED OTHER-SPECIFY)	1 PROTESTANT 2 BAPTIST 3 EPISCOPALIAN 4 LUTHERAN 5 METHODIST 6 PRESBYTERIAN 7 ROMAN CATHOLIC 8 JEWISH 9 OTHER	
INT CHECK 79 - IS R IN THE MILITARY SAMPLE?	1 if yes, 0 otherwise	R01500.00
EVER LIVED OUTSIDE HOME OF PARENTS FOR > 1 MONTH SINCE JAN 1978?	1 if yes, 0 otherwise	R01502.00
SEX OF R	1 if male, 2 if female	R02148.00
MARITAL STATUS	1 NEVER MARRIED 2 MARRIED 3 SEPARATED 4 DIVORCED 5 WIDOWED	R70070.00
HIGHEST GRADE COMPLETED AS OF MAY 1 SURVEY YEAR	0 NONE 93 PRE-KINDERGARTEN 94 KINDERGARTEN 1 1ST GRADE 2 2ND GRADE 3 3RD GRADE 4 4TH GRADE 5 5TH GRADE 6 6TH GRADE 7 7TH GRADE 8 8TH GRADE 9 9TH GRADE 10 10TH GRADE 11 11TH GRADE 12 12TH GRADE 13 1ST YEAR COLLEGE 14 2ND YEAR COLLEGE 15 3RD YEAR COLLEGE 16 4TH YEAR COLLEGE 17 5TH YEAR COLLEGE 18 6TH YEAR COLLEGE	R70071.00

Variable Name	Description	Variable Code
	19 7TH YEAR COLLEGE	
	20 8TH YEAR COLLEGE OR MORE	
IS R's CURRENT	0: RURAL	R70089.00
RESIDENCE	1: URBAN	
URBAN/RURAL? (2000)	2: UNKNOWN	

From the variables above, we created a series of dummy variables, including the following:

SINGLE	1 if R has never been married, 0 otherwise
MARRIED	1 if R is married, 0 otherwise
SEPARATED	1 if R is separated, 0 otherwise
DIVORCED	1 if R is divorced, 0 otherwise
WIDOWED	1 if R is widowed, 0 otherwise
BLACK	1 if R is black, 0 otherwise
ASIAN	1 if R is an Asian or Pacific Island American, 0 otherwise
NATIVE_AM	1 if R is a Native American, 0 otherwise
HISPANIC	1 if R is a Hispanic, 0 otherwise
RACE_OTHER	1 if R identifies as an unincluded race, 0 otherwise
WHITE	1 if R is white, 0 otherwise
PROTESTANT	1 if R was raised a Protestant, 0 otherwise
ROM_CATH	1 if R was raised a Roman Catholic, 0 otherwise
JEWISH	1 if R was raised Jewish, 0 otherwise
REL_OTHER	1 if R was raised in another religion, 0 otherwise
NO_REL	1 if R was raised without religion, 0 otherwise
LIVE_BOTH	1 if R lived with both of his parents, 0 otherwise
LIVE_DAD_OTH	1 if R lived with his father and another woman, 0 otherwise
LIVE_DAD	1 if R lived with his father only, 0 otherwise
LIVE_MOM_OTH	1 if R lived with his mother and another man, 0 otherwise
LIVE_MOM	1 if R lived with his mother only, 0 otherwise
LIVE_OTHER	1 if R lived with neither his father or mother, 0 otherwise

ESTIMATION PROCEDURE

While the NLSY provides a detailed set of variables, allowing us to capture many of characteristics of individuals that may affect their income, it suffers from considerable problems of missing data. That is, for many individuals included in the study, data are not available for important variables in every period of interest. Statistical analyses of data sets such as the NLSY have often employed listwise deletion to address this problem. Listwise deletion simply indicates that the analyst drops observations with missing values from the statistical analysis employed. While often considered benign, King et al. (2001) show that listwise deletion introduces systematic bias and inefficiency into parameter estimates unless the missing data are "Missing Completely at Random" (see also Rubin 1977). In the present analysis of the NLSY, it is likely that there are unobserved but systematic factors that influence the probability that respondents' information is available. It is probable, for example, that respondents with lower incomes are less likely to be contacted after twenty years than respondents with higher incomes. Similarly, certain religious groups may be less likely to answer certain questions on the NLSY than other religious groups. Unless there are *no* systematic factors that affect the probability that data are missing from our sample, listwise deletion is an inappropriate method for dealing with missing data. We consider it highly unlikely that missing data in the NLSY are Missing Completely at Random. The Amelia software by Honaker et al. (2001) allows us to simply and efficiently employ a multiple imputation algorithm to address these issues (see discussion in Schafer 1997; King et al. 2001). Using this software, we generate simulated data sets that avoid the issues of missing data in our sample from the NLSY, and run our statistical tests on them. All of our analyses were performed in Stata, version 8.

We regress our dependent variable, the natural logarithm of an individual's income, on our array of independent variables. In our first model, we employ OLS regression, using our different measures of the dependent variable. The results from these three regressions are presented as Tables 6.1, 6.2, and 6.3 in the body of Chapter 6.

We suspect, however, that the effects of our independent variables on the dependent variable vary across values of the dependent variable. Following the suggestions of Koenker and Hallock (2001), we therefore re-estimate our parameter coefficients across a number of different income groups, employing the method of quantile regression. If OLS regression estimates the sample mean of the dependent variable, conditional on values of the independent variable, then median regression – the special case of quantile regression for the median observation of the dependent variable – estimates the sample median conditional on the values of the independent variable. This works though minimizing the sum of absolute residuals from the regression plane, rather than the sum of the squared residuals, as in the case of OLS regression. A similar procedure can separate data into any quantiles conditional on the independent variables (see Buchinsky 1998; Koenker and Hallock 2001). We explored differential effects of our independent variables of interest for the tenth percentile (0.1 quantile), first quartile (0.25 quantile), median (0.5 quantile), third quartile (0.75 quantile), and ninetieth percentile (0.9 quantile) of the data. Our results remain substantively unchanged, and no major differential effects are apparent across groups.

Finally, we check for robustness by clustering our observations by the SMSA in which the individual lives. Heretofore, we have assumed that all of our observations are independent from one another. However, if there are factors specific to each SMSA that affect each individual's income, then this assumption is invalid – the disturbances will be uncorrelated between SMSAs, but will be correlated among SMSAs. Clustering our observations by SMSAs allows us to obtain consistent estimates of our standard errors while specifically allowing for non-independence of observations within SMSAs. Unfortunately, the problem of missing data is particularly acute in the case of the individual's SMSA, so much so that our imputation algorithm does not converge. Despite our reservations about the randomness of missing observations, we proceed by dropping individuals with missing SMSA information from our analysis, but continue to use our imputed data sets.

The following regressions re-estimate the first three models, clustering by SMSA and dropping observations where SMSA components were missing.

Thomas Pepinsky

Multiple Imputation Estimates
Model: regress
Dependent Variable: log_avg_ws
Number of Observations: 3866

	Coef.	Std. Err.	t	Df	P>|t|
son_age	.00828	.0078097	1.060	67868	0.289
dad_age	.00131	.0028993	0.453	23	0.655
log_fam_inc	.18932	.041806	4.528	46	0.000
log_educ_exp	.10662	.0101515	10.503	14	0.000
log_avg_educ	−.10359	.2190314	−0.473	32	0.639
south	−.09239	.0477174	−1.936	13	0.075
foreign_lang	−.06515	.0518421	−1.257	844	0.209
sibs	−.01425	.0089776	−1.587	17	0.131
military	.27252	.14132	1.928	44	0.060
outside_home	−.1654	.0794874	−2.081	13	0.057
urban	.07595	.0396271	1.917	45	0.062
married	.70811	.0430281	16.457	264	0.000
separated	.27798	.0948262	2.931	179	0.004
divorced	.3262	.0552262	5.907	402	0.000
widowed	.65213	.2240607	2.911	50	0.005
live_dad_other_woman	−.09964	.1263633	−0.788	62	0.433
live_dad	−.24133	.1781727	−1.354	30	0.186
live_mom_other_man	−.1251	.0962305	−1.300	12	0.218
live_mom	−.06638	.0641837	−1.034	18	0.315
live_other	−.09886	.0867691	−1.139	42	0.261
black	−.27287	.0448933	−6.078	97	0.000
asian	.18356	.1394725	1.316	35	0.197
native_am	−.09817	.0859753	−1.142	47	0.259
hispanic	−.08304	.0688218	−1.207	165	0.229
race_other	−.02192	.0509782	−0.430	106	0.668
protestant	.07801	.0832288	0.937	22	0.359
rom_cath	.12176	.0943748	1.290	13	0.219
jewish	.26462	.1585152	1.669	13	0.119
other_rel	.00607	.0865673	0.070	31	0.945
_cons	8.8112	2.204906	3.996	38	0.000

Multiple Imputation Estimates

Model: regress

Dependent Variable: log_avg_ws_fb

Number of Observations: 3866

	Coef.	Std. Err.	t	Df	P>|t|
son_age	.00688	.0079944	0.861	7781	0.389
dad_age	.00225	.0030956	0.726	18	0.477
log_fam_inc	.20437	.0455984	4.482	31	0.000
log_educ_exp	.10288	.0106109	9.695	15	0.000
log_avg_educ	−.02966	.2265001	−0.131	28	0.897
south	−.1063	.0491497	−2.163	13	0.050
foreign_lang	−.06292	.0536684	−1.172	5495	0.241
sibs	−.01579	.0086478	−1.826	18	0.085
military	.25211	.1573298	1.602	22	0.123
outside_home	−.14851	.0775046	−1.916	12	0.079
urban	.06827	.0393009	1.737	45	0.089
married	.70513	.0430881	16.365	523	0.000
separated	.26346	.0960855	2.742	163	0.007
divorced	.32263	.055993	5.762	319	0.000
widowed	.64395	.2326971	2.767	40	0.009
live_dad_other_woman	−.12591	.1409172	−0.893	29	0.379
live_dad	−.25492	.1742198	−1.463	30	0.154
live_mom_other_man	−.12004	.1058967	−1.134	9	0.285
live_mom	−.05917	.0645749	−0.916	22	0.369
live_other	−.07967	.0905532	−0.880	43	0.384
black	−.30563	.0420378	−7.270	208	0.000
asian	.1729	.147786	1.170	26	0.253
native_am	−.11687	.084928	−1.376	63	0.174
hispanic	−.0964	.0720812	−1.337	167	0.183
race_other	−.03451	.0526488	−0.656	83	0.514
protestant	.07377	.0777159	0.949	41	0.348
rom_cath	.08937	.0888008	1.006	17	0.329
jewish	.24321	.1379046	1.764	29	0.088
other_rel	−.00279	.0833926	−0.033	42	0.973
_cons	8.0908	2.289298	3.534	32	0.001

Multiple Imputation Estimates

Model: regress
Dependent Variable: log_avg_net

Number of Observations: 3866

	Coef.	Std. Err.	t	Df	P>|t|
son_age	.01278	.0084343	1.515	27	0.141
dad_age	.00025	.0028426	0.089	11	0.931
log_fam_inc	.18739	.0526509	3.559	11	0.004
log_educ_exp	.0914	.0073439	12.446	1798	0.000
log_avg_educ	−.04015	.1675576	−0.240	980	0.811
south	−.07371	.0389721	−1.891	24	0.071
foreign_lang	−.05344	.0537178	−0.995	33	0.327
sibs	−.02301	.007485	−3.074	19	0.006
military	.30923	.181137	1.707	14	0.109
outside_home	−.11505	.0528325	−2.178	44	0.035
urban	.03161	.0360759	0.876	189	0.382
married	.85383	.0401512	21.265	88	0.000
separated	.31441	.0887567	3.542	99	0.001
divorced	.31115	.0624798	4.980	19	0.000
widowed	.09208	.282889	0.326	74	0.746
live_dad_other_woman	−.0583	.1367516	−0.426	57	0.671
live_dad	−.10398	.15679	−0.663	13	0.519
live_mom_other_man	−.07319	.0933645	−0.784	9	0.454
live_mom	−.02391	.0548824	−0.436	45	0.665
live_other	−.15024	.0770586	−1.950	153	0.053
black	−.21572	.0474514	−4.546	23	0.000
asian	.0474	.1532953	0.309	57	0.758
native_am	−.08996	.0935828	−0.961	74	0.340
hispanic	−.05372	.0544377	−0.987	632	0.324
race_other	.00753	.0481359	0.156	105	0.876
protestant	.0694	.1125856	0.616	9	0.553
rom_cath	.07862	.1098026	0.716	10	0.491
jewish	.18382	.1524025	1.206	24	0.240
other_rel	.02715	.1056324	0.257	13	0.801
_cons	8.6512	1.74331	4.963	666	0.000

CHAPTER 7

Conclusion

A. A REVIEW OF OUR APPROACH

Our project has been to endogenize society's investment in the human capital of its citizens through modeling the political process of democratic competition. On the economic side, we initially chose an educational production function in which the human capital of the worker is determined by the human capital of his or her parents and the amount invested in his or her education. Later, we generalized this, and included the effect on the individual worker's human capital – or rather, his or her earnings – of the average human capital of his or her cohort, where 'cohort' can have either of two interpretations: those with whom he or she attended school, or those with whom he or she works. (In our model, these two groups are identical because only one generation of workers comprises the labor force at any given time; a more highly articulated model would distinguish between these two senses of cohort.)

On the political side, we constructed a model of party competition in which two parties form and compete on an infinite-dimensional space of policies, where a policy specifies precisely the taxes paid by every household, the transfers the household receives, and the amount invested by the state in the education of every child. We argued that the large policy space was necessary to model ruthless competition between parties – we might have also said realistic competition. Indeed, we later showed that it makes a difference to work on the large policy space because the results in a more traditional, unidimensional Downsian model are quite different from what occurs in our model.

A voter's type was characterized by his or her human capital or wage; this sufficed to determine his or her preferences over policies. Because the distribution of wages of the next generation is determined by political decisions of the current generation, once we specify a theory of political competition in the current period, we determine the distribution of types in the next period, up to the outcome of an election with a stochastic element, and hence the political equilibrium of the next period. This sets in motion a stochastic dynamic process, which allows us to study the asymptotic properties of the distribution of human capital.

There were two complications: first of all, our theory of equilibrium produces not a unique equilibrium, but a two-dimensional manifold of equilibria at every date. Thus, in our dynamic study, we elected to examine two kinds of dynamic equilibrium path: one in which politics are extremely ideological, and the other in which they are extremely opportunist. The second complication was that, in our model, elections are uncertain, and so a political equilibrium specifies not which policy wins, but rather a lottery on pairs of policies.

In our dynamic analysis, we took as a benchmark the dynamics of a laissez-faire economy, in which there is no taxation and each household allocates its resources between consumption and private educational investment. We observed that the dynamics crucially depend upon the nature of scale economies in the educational production function. We argued that the case of constant returns to scale $(b + c = 1)$ was the interesting case to study because it provides the sharpest possible contrast between the benchmark case and democracy with a redistributive state. In particular it allows us to separate the effects of political competition on the tendency, or otherwise, to equality, from the effects of technology.

Our central results were the following: first, in an intertemporal sequence of quasi-PUNEs where the probability of victory remains constant over time, and in which politics are as opportunist as possible at each date, the coefficient of variation of the distribution of earnings decreases in the limit to a positive number. Thus, the effect of a dynasty's initial endowment, the human capital of its primeval Eve, remains persistent forever on the human capital of its members.

On the other hand, if politics are at each date extremely ideological, we could not derive complete analytical results. If the pivot voter is sufficiently rich, we proved that, asymptotically, the coefficient of variation is positive. Based on simulations, we are confident in asserting that, if the pivot voter is sufficiently poor, then there is a positive probability that the process does converge to equality of human capital. That probability, however, is generally less than one.

For sequences of equilibria that do not lie on the boundaries of the equilibrium manifold, the results should be less extreme than what occurs on the boundary.

In conclusion, we are confident in asserting that in any sequence of quasi-PUNEs where the pivot remains in the same dynasty at every date, there is at least a positive probability, which may be unity, that the process *does not* converge to equality. Democracy does not *surely* engender equality.

Although the model we analyzed assumed that no variation in talent or effort existed among the children of the tranche of parents with the same human capital, we may conjecture about the dynamics with that amendment to the model. With a stochastic talent or effort term, there is never convergence to a zero coefficient of variation. What we conjecture occurs is that, with opportunist politics, the persistence of the dynasty's initial endowment remains forever on the earnings of its future members, whereas with ideological politics, there is, with positive probability, no such persistence. If we conceive of equality of opportunity as a state in which a worker's earnings are determined only by his or her own effort and not by characteristics of his or her dynasty, then we can say that ideological politics may engender, at least in the limit, a state of equality of opportunity, while opportunist politics surely do not.

One important fact about the first model we analyzed is that it provides no understanding of why educational finance in all democracies is largely public. We showed that citizens were indifferent between public and private financing of education in that model. Our equilibrium model does determine the distribution of human capital at each date (*modulo* the multiplicity issue) but it does not determine the division of educational finance between private and public. We argued that this was a consequence of our first educational production function, in which returns to education are entirely private. We consequently modified the production function in Chapter 5 to capture an externality, as we described earlier.

Our results are if the externality is sufficiently important (in the sense of a large enough ratio d/c), then even in the case of opportunist politics, the coefficient of variation of human capital tends to zero. *A fortiori*, we presume (although we offered no proof) that, at *any* sequence of equilibria in which the probability of victory of the parties remains constant, wages will tend to equality. We also observed that with endogenous growth, we can understand why educational finance is public: political competition solves a free rider problem. Every household would like a large investment in education, and Pareto efficiency requires that more is invested in his or her child than the individual household head would like to invest, *given* the total resources that are allocated to his or her household in the political equilibrium.

Because our dynamic results are sensitive to the sizes of the three elasticities b, c, and d, we finally attempted some econometric estimation of these values, using data from the United States. We found that $b > c$ and $b + c < 1$; we were unable to estimate d. If we think it is reasonable that technical innovation depends on the education and skill of the labor force, in two senses (that more educated labor will innovate more and that more sophisticated technology can be employed with more educated labor) then it is likely that d is positive. We cannot conjecture the size of the ratio d/c, which is critical for the dynamic analysis of Chapter 5.

B. LIMITATIONS OF THE MODEL

I will discuss six limitations of the model, beyond and above the ones I have already alluded to in the quick review:

- incentive effects
- exogenous shocks

- racial/immigration issues
- imperfectly representative democracy
- multi-party politics
- altruism

1. Incentive Effects

Two kinds of incentive effect have been ignored: children do not take account of how hard they should work in school, due to the likely taxation on their income in the next period, and adults do not reduce their labor supply in response to taxation. I have not modeled these effects because my attempts to include them have rendered the model intractable. (As mentioned earlier, they transform well-behaved concave optimization programs into non-concave programs.) We note that these effects are potentially important because in our model, where they are ignored, there are substantial parts of the income distribution in which the marginal tax rate is 100 percent in the equilibrium policies of both parties.

It seems intuitively clear that incentive effects will slow down or perhaps stop altogether the convergence of wages to equality. Hence, were incentive effects included, the case to study would be one of extremely ideological politics. Would convergence to equality of wages still occur with positive probability in that case?

2. Exogenous Shocks

The divergence of skilled from unskilled wages in certain advanced democracies in the recent period is due, let us say, to technological changes that our model does not contemplate. How important are such events in history? I do not know.

3. Racial/Immigration Issues

Our model has assumed that citizens differ only according to their human capital, and that political competition is concerned only with distribution, not with other issues. In reality, issues of race and immigration are important in advanced democracies. Indeed, there is strong evidence that racism in the United States has considerably reduced the degree of redistribution below what it would have been in its absence (see Lee and Roemer [in press]). One can predict that something similar will occur in Europe as European countries come to depend more upon immigrant labor due to the decline in fertility. Indeed, it may not be a coincidence that the most homogeneous democracies (with regard to language, race, and religion) are the most egalitarian ones: the Nordic countries.

4. Imperfectly Representative Democracy

In our model, each citizen belongs to one party, and each party has a utility function that reflects the interests of its members in proportion to their numbers. Representation is thus 'perfect' in two ways: one person one vote in the election, and one person one vote in the intra-party preference formation process. In reality, democracies only approach these desiderata to varying degrees. In the United States, where private campaign contributions play a large role, one cannot expect that the intra-party preference formation process conforms to the one-person-one-vote desideratum.

In our model of perfectly representative democracy, the membership of the party is co-extensive with the set of those who vote for the party. With privately financed election campaigns, these two sets of citizens diverge. Although the modeling of political competition with privately financed parties is in its infancy, enough has been done to indicate that the members of a party – taken to be its set of contributors – and those who vote for it are two different sets of people.[1]

Indeed, preliminary work indicates that with private campaign finance in a two-party system, there will emerge endogenously two parties, one that represents a fairly small fraction of citizens at the top of the wealth distribution, and the other that represents everyone else. (See Roemer [2003]). Nevertheless, both parties are viable, in the sense of having positive probabilities of victory. It is not too hard to see that, in this situation, politics are shifted unambiguously to the right: clearly the small party of the wealthy does not desire redistribution, and because the other party represents everyone else, it too will be quite moderate.

---

[1] See the survey paper by Morton and Cameron (1992), and Roemer (2003) for a political equilibrium model with private campaign and endogenous parties.

Whether, in this situation, convergence to equality of wages will ever occur is, thus far, an unstudied problem. It is possible, however, that the days of privately financed elections are numbered, and that within a century or two all parties will be publicly financed, and consequently parties will come to reflect the interests of those who vote for them rather than the interests of their private contributors.

5. Multi-party Political Competition

Our model posits that precisely two parties will form. In most democracies this is not the case. I have not modeled multi-party politics here because it is more complex. With more than two parties, political competition must be modeled as (at least) a two-stage game. In the first stage, parties form and an election occurs. In the second stage, a coalition government is formed, assuming that no party has won a majority of votes. Voters must take into account the second stage when voting in the first stage. It follows that the rational voter should be strategic rather than sincere: he or she does not always vote for the party whose policy he or she prefers, as it may be better to vote for another party that has a greater probability of being involved in the coalition government.

There is very little consensus among political scientists on how to model this second stage; this is an additional reason to first study the two-party model whose basic structure is more established.

Still, there is some reason to suppose that multi-party politics will be more equalizing than two-party politics. Austen-Smith (2000) reaches this conclusion. It is therefore perhaps the case that the two-party problem is the most conservative one to analyze, with regard to egalitarian concerns.

6. Altruism

We have assumed that voters are interested only in the welfare of their own dynasty. In reality, voters are interested in the welfare of other children as well. Indeed, an important effect of racism and xenophobia is that it prevents altruism across racial or ethnic groups. The Nordic societies, the most egalitarian in the world today, are also the most homogeneous ones – or were during the period in which large social insurance programs were enacted.

Changing the utility function to make voters care about the welfare of other peoples' children will have a similar effect to putting the externality in the educational production function as discussed in Chapter 5. Therefore, one way of interpreting our results is to say that, *absent altruism*, there is no guarantee that democracy, conceived of as ruthless but peaceful political competition, will engender equality.

C. WHY HAS CONVERGENCE TO EQUALITY OF WAGES NOT BEEN MORE RAPID?

Our theory, and these comments, perhaps provide sufficient explanation for the non-convergence to equality of human capital in the advanced democracies.[2] Even the advanced democracies have only had universal suffrage for approximately one century. In reality, talent and effort do vary within the tranche of households with parents of the same socio-economic status, so we should not expect equality of wages asymptotically in any case, but only lack of persistence. On this count, advanced democracies might appear to be performing quite well. Clearly, it is beyond the scope of this publication to study the inter-generational mobility literature. The rapidly developed and massive present importance of publicly financed education, in the historical period of democracy, is certainly consistent with our model. There are the so-called exogenous shocks. There are the incentive effects of taxation that, as I said, our model has ignored. Democracies have porous borders, and are constantly importing new citizens who come from undemocratic states, and whose level of human capital is low.

D. A FINAL NOTE

A growth modeler must possess hubris to believe that his or her model has really got it right; small errors in the conceptualization can, over time, have large effects on asymptotic results – this is, if you wish, a

---

[2] Castello and Domenech (2002) do find that the coefficients of variation of the distributions of human capital are converging in a large number of countries.

methodological version of the principle of compound interest. Political economy is in its infancy, as I said earlier, an infancy reflected in our not being able to analyze models that are sufficiently complex on both the economic and political sides. I have elected, in this publication, to articulate the political side in relatively great detail, and to simplify the economic side. Who knows if this is the right choice? At least we now know that the choice matters, in the sense that the simple Hotelling-Downs model of politics does not give the same results as the model of parties conceived as factions.

I certainly lack the required hubris; the most I would hope is that this work will be a stepping stone for future researchers who are concerned with this important question. For if equality of opportunity is the most accepted conception of justice in democratic societies – and if democracy with competitive, endogenous parties is our chosen political institution for the next several centuries at least – then every social scientist should be interested in whether democratic political competition will engender that kind of equality.

References

Aldrich, John. 1995. *Why Parties?* Chicago: University of Chicago Press.

Artémeadis, N. K. 1976. *Real Analysis*, Carbondale: Southern Illinois University Press.

Austen-Smith, D. 2000. "Redistributing income with proportional representation," *Journal of Political Economy* 108, 1235–1269.

Baron, D. 1993. "Government formation and endogenous parties," *American Political Science Review* 87, 34–47.

Bénabou, R. 1996. "Heterogeneity, stratification, and growth: Macroeconomic implications of community structure and school finance," *American Economic Review* 86, 584–609.

Besley, T. and S. Coate, 1997. "An economic model of representative democracy," *Quarterly Journal of Economics* 90, 85–114.

Bourgignon, F. and T. Verdier, 2000. "Oligarchy, democracy, inequality and growth," *Journal of Development Economics* 62, 285–313.

Buchinsky, Moshe. 1998. "Recent Advances in Quantile Regression: A Practical Guide for Empirical Research." *Journal of Human Resources* 33(1), pp. 88–126.

Caplin, A. and B. Nalebuff, 1997. "Competition among institutions," *Journal of Economic Theory* 72, 306–342.

Cardak, B. 1999. "Heterogeneous preferences, education expenditures and income distribution," *Economic Record* 75, 63–76.

Castello, A. and R. Domenech, 2002. "Human capital inequality and economic growth: Some new evidence," *Economic Journal* 112, C187–200.

Downs, A. 1957. *An economic theory of democracy*, New York: Harper-Collins.

Durlauf, S. 1996. "A theory of persistent income inequality," *Journal of Economic Growth* 1, 75–93.

Epple, D. and T. Romer, 1991. "Mobility and redistribution," *Journal of Political Economy* 99, 828–858.

Fernández, R. and R. Rogerson, 1998. "Public education and income distribution: A dynamic quantitative evaluation of education-finance reform," *American Economic Review* 88, 813–833.

Glomm, G. and B. Ravikumar, 2003. "Public education and income inequality," *European Journal of Political Economy* 19, 289–300.

Gomberg, A. M., F. Marhuenda, and I. Ortuño-Ortin, 2004. "A model of endogenous political party platforms," *Economic Theory* 24, 373–394.

Gradstein, M. and M. Justman, 1996. "The political economy of mixed public and private schooling: A dynamic analysis," *International Tax and Public Finance* 3, 297–310.

Hardy, G. H., J. E. Littlewood, and G. Pólya, 1964. *Inequalities*, Cambridge: Cambridge University Press.

Hinich, M. J. and M. C. Munger, 1997. *Analytical Politics*, New York: Cambridge University Press.

Honaker, James, Anne Joseph, Gary King, Kenneth Scheve, and Naunihal Singh. 2001. Amelia: *A Program for Missing Data* (Windows version). Cambridge, MA: Harvard University, *http://GKing.Harvard.edu/*.

Hotelling, H. 1929. "Stability in competition," *Economic Journal* 39, 41–57.

King, Gary, James Honaker, Anne Joseph, and Kenneth Scheve. 2001. "Analyzing Incomplete Political Science Data." *American Political Science Review* 95(1), pp. 49–69.

Klingermann, Hans-Dieter, Richard Hofferbert, and Ian Budge, 1994. *Parties, Policies, and Democracy*. Boulder, CO: Westview Press.

Koenker, Roger and Kevin F. Hallock, 2001. "Quantile regression," *Journal of Economic Perspectives* 15(4), pp. 143–156.

Krehbiel, K. 1993. "Where's the Party?" *British Journal of Political Science*, 23, 235–266.

Lee, W. and J. Roemer, in press. "Racism and distribution in American politics: A solution to the problem of American exceptionalism," *Journal of Public Economics*.

Lindahl, E. [1919] 1958. "Just taxation – a positive solution," in Musgrave and Peacock.

Lipset, S. M. [1960] 1994. *Political Man*, Baltimore: Johns Hopkins University Press.

Morton, R. and C. Cameron, 1992. "Elections and the theory of campaign contributions: A suvery and critical analysis," *Economics & Politics* 4, 79–108.

Musgrave, R. and A. Peacock (eds.) 1958. *Classics in the Theory of Public Finance*, New York and London: Macmillan.

National Longitudinal Study of Youth. 2000. US Department of Labor, Bureau of Labor Statistics.

Osborne, M. and A. Slivinski, 1996. "A model of political competition with citizen-candidates," *Quarterly Journal of Economics* 91, 65–96.

Persson, T. and G. Tabellini, 1994. "Is inequality harmful for growth?" *American Economic Review* 84, 600–621.

Przeworski, A. 1999. "Minimalist theory of democracy: A defence," in I. Shapiro and C. Hacker-Cordon (eds.), *Democracy's Value*, Cambridge University Press.

Roemer, J. E. 1996. *Theories of Distributive Justice*, Cambridge, MA: Harvard University Press.

Roemer, J. E. 1998. *Equality of Opportunity*, Cambridge, MA: Harvard University Press.

Roemer, J. E. 1999. "The democratic political economy of progressive taxation," *Econometrica* 67, 1–19.

Roemer, J. E. 2001. *Political Competition*, Cambridge, MA: Harvard University Press.

Roemer, J. E. 2003. "Political equilibrium with private and/or public campaign finance: A comparison of institutions," Yale University, Cowles Discussion Paper No. 1409.

Roemer, J. E. 2005. "Distribution and politics: A brief history and prospect," *Social Choice and Welfare*.

Rubin, Donald. 1977. "Formalizing Subjective Notions about the Effect of Nonrespondents in Sample Surveys." *Journal of the American Statistical Association* 72, pp. 538–543.

Saint-Paul, G. and T. Verdier, 1993. "Education, democracy and growth," *Journal of Development Economics* 42, 399–407.

Schafer, Joseph L. 1997. *Analysis of Incomplete Multivariate Data*. London: Chapman and Hall.

Schorske, Carl. [1955] 1993. *German Social Democracy:1905–1917*, Cambridge MA: Harvard University Press.

Turrini, A. 1998. "Endogenous education policy and increasing income inequality between skilled and unskilled workers," *European Journal of Political Economy* 14, 303–326.

Wittman, D. 1973. "Parties as utility maximizers," *American Political Science Review* 67, 490–498.

Zhang, J. 1996. "Optimal public investments in education and endogenous growth," *Scandinavian Journal of Economics* 98, 387–404.

Appendix: Proofs of Theorems

CHAPTER 3

1. Solution of Program (SL1)

To solve:

$$\max_{X \in T^*} \int_0^{h^*} \log X(h) d\mathbf{F}(h)$$

$$s.t.$$

$$0 \le X'(h) \le 1$$

$$\int X(h) d\mathbf{F}(h) = \mu$$

We give an intuitive argument.[1] The solution must be the constant function $X^L(h) = \mu$. Suppose the solution were anywhere increasing in the interval $[0, h^*]$. By shifting resources from types who receive more to types who receive less, the value of the objective would increase because it is concave. Clearly, the solution must be constant on (h^*, ∞) because it cannot be decreasing, but there is no value to giving any resource to those types. The budget constraint thus implies that the solution is as stated.

Therefore $y^L(h^*) = \mu$.

---

[1] A rigorous proof can easily be supplied, following the technique of paragraph 3 below.

2. Solution of Program (SL2)

To solve:

$$\max_{X(\cdot)} X(h^*)$$

$s.t.$

$$0 \le X'(h) \le 1$$

$$\int X(h)d\mathbf{F}(h) = \mu$$

The solution is:

$$X^*(h) = \begin{cases} X_0^* + h, & 0 \le h \le h^* \\ X_0^* + h^*, & h > h^* \end{cases}$$

where X_0^* is the solution of the equation:

$$X_0^* + \int_0^{h^*} hd\mathbf{F}(h) + h^*(1 - F(h^*)) = \mu. \tag{A3.1}$$

We offer again an intuitive argument. Clearly, X must be constant for $h > h^*$. On the other hand, X should decrease as rapidly as possible to the left of h^* because giving resources to all types other than h^* is a waste. Thus the solution has a slope of one to the left of h^*. The budget constraint thus takes the form of (A3.1), which characterizes the solution. Note that $h^* > 0$ implies that $X_0^* > 0$ as long as $F(h^*) < 1$.

3. Solution of Program (SR1)

$$\max_{X(\cdot)} \int_{h^*}^{\infty} \log X(h)d\mathbf{F}(h)$$

$s.t.$

$$0 \le X'(h) \le 1$$

$$\int X(h)d\mathbf{F}(h) = \mu$$

The solution is given by:

$$X^R(h) = \begin{cases} x + h, & \text{for } h \le y \\ x + y, & \text{for } h > y \end{cases}$$

where (x, y) solves the following two simultaneous equations:

$$x + \int_0^y h\, d\mathbf{F}(h) + y(1 - F(y)) = \mu \tag{A3.2a}$$

$$\int_{h^*}^y \frac{d\mathbf{F}(h)}{h + x} = \frac{F(y)}{x + y}. \tag{A3.2b}$$

Proof: (A3.2a) says that the function X^R integrates to μ, as required; (A3.2b) fixes a particular pair of numbers (x, y).

Denote this policy by X^*, for short.

Here we introduce a method for solving the various optimization problems that we shall use henceforth. The method amounts to finding shadow prices for the various constraints.

Suppose, contrary to the claim, that X^* is not the solution to the program; rather, the solution is $X(h) = X^*(h) + g(h)$, where g is some non-zero function. Our method will be to derive a contradiction to this claim.

For a non-negative function λ defined on the interval $[0, y]$ and a positive number δ, and for any function g, define the function

$$\Delta(\varepsilon) = \int_{h^*}^{\infty} Log(X^*(h) + \varepsilon g(h)) d F(h)$$

$$+ \int_0^y \lambda(h)(1 - (X^*(h) + \varepsilon g(h))') dh$$

$$+ \delta \left(\mu - \int_0^{\infty} (X^*(h) + \varepsilon g(h)) d F(h) \right).$$

I will produce a function λ and a number δ such that, for any function g, Δ is maximized at $\varepsilon = 0$. In particular, it will follow that $\Delta(0) \geq \Delta(1)$.

Observe that the second and third terms on the r.h.s. of the definition of Δ vanish at $\varepsilon = 0$. Observe also that if $X^* + g$ is feasible, then the second and third terms on the r.h.s. of the definition of Δ are non-negative at $\varepsilon = 1$. Hence we will have:

$$\int_{h^*}^{\infty} Log\, X^*(h)\, dF(h) \geq \int_{h^*}^{\infty} Log(X^*(h) + g(h))\, dF(h),$$

for the variation g, contradicting the claim that X gives a higher value to the objective than X^*.

Note that Δ is a concave function.[2] It therefore suffices to show that $\Delta'(0) = 0$. Define λ and δ as follows, where f is the density of $\mathbf{F}$ and (x, y) are defined above:

   (i) $\lambda(0) = 0$,
   (ii) $\lambda'(h) = \delta f(h)$ on $[0, h^*]$,
   (iii) $\lambda'(h) = \delta f(h) - \frac{f(h)}{h+x}$ on $[h^*, y]$,
   (iv) $\lambda(y) = 0$, and
   (v) $\delta = \frac{1}{x+y}$.

We must show that (i)–(iv) are consistent, given (v). Note that $\lambda' \geq 0$ on $[0, h^*]$ from (ii) and $\lambda' \leq 0$ on $[h^*, y]$ from (iii) and (v). From (i), (ii), and (v):

$$\lambda(h^*) = \int_0^{h^*} \delta f(h)\, dh = \frac{F(h^*)}{x+y}.$$

From (iii):

$$\lambda(y) - \lambda(h^*) = \int_{h^*}^{y} f(h) \left(\frac{1}{x+y} - \frac{1}{h+x} \right) dh.$$

Therefore (iv) is true if

$$0 - \frac{F(h^*)}{x+y} = \int_{h^*}^{y} \left(\frac{1}{x+y} - \frac{1}{h+x} \right) f(h)\, dh$$

$$= \frac{F(y) - F(h^*)}{x+y} - \int_{h^*}^{y} \frac{d\mathbf{F}(h)}{h+x},$$

---

[2] This key step is where we exploit the fact that the optimization program is concave.

which is true if and only if:

$$\int\limits_{h^*}^{y} \frac{d\mathbf{F}(h)}{h+x} = \frac{F(y)}{x+y}.$$

But the last equation is true by definition of (x, y).

Thus the function λ is well-defined and non-negative on its domain, as required.

We now differentiate Δ, where g is an arbitrary, (almost everywhere) differentiable function:

$$\Delta'(0) = \int\limits_{h^*}^{\infty} \frac{g(h)d\mathbf{F}(h)}{X^*(h)} - \int\limits_{0}^{y} \lambda(h)g'(h) - \delta \int\limits_{0}^{\infty} g(h)d\mathbf{F}(h)$$

$$= \int\limits_{h^*}^{y} \frac{g(h)d\mathbf{F}(h)}{h+x} + \int\limits_{y}^{\infty} \frac{g(h)d\mathbf{F}(h)}{x+y} + \int\limits_{0}^{h^*} \lambda'(h)g(h)dh$$

$$+ \int\limits_{h^*}^{y} \lambda'(h)g(h)dh - \lambda(h)g(h)\Big|_{0}^{y} - \delta \int\limits_{0}^{h^*} g(h)d\mathbf{F}(h)$$

$$- \delta \int\limits_{h^*}^{\infty} g(h)d\mathbf{F}(h)$$

where we used integration by parts,

$$= \int\limits_{h^*}^{y} \left(\frac{f(h)}{h+x} + \lambda'(h) \right) g(h)dh + \left(\frac{1}{x+y} - \delta \right) \int\limits_{y}^{\infty} g(h)d\mathbf{F}(h)$$

$$- \delta \int\limits_{h^*}^{y} g(h)d\mathbf{F}(h) + \int\limits_{0}^{h^*} (\lambda'(h) - \delta f(h))g(h)dh - \lambda(y)g(y) + \lambda(0)g(0)$$

$$= \int\limits_{h^*}^{y} \left(\frac{f(h)}{h+x} + \lambda'(h) - \delta f(h) \right) g(h)dh + \left(\frac{1}{x+y} - \delta \right)$$

$$\times \int\limits_{y}^{\infty} g(h)d\mathbf{F}(h) + \int\limits_{0}^{h^*} (\lambda'(h) - \delta f(h))g(h)dh + 0$$

$$= [\text{by definition of } \lambda' \text{ and } \delta] \quad 0,$$

as was to be shown.

We finally prove that $x > 0$. Using integration by parts:

$$\int_0^y h \, d\mathbf{F}(h) = hF(h)\big|_0^y - \int_0^y F(h)dh = yF(h) - \int_0^y F(h)dh.$$

Hence, (A3.2a) reduces to

$$x = \mu + \int_0^y F(h)dh - y = \mu + \int_0^y (1 - F(h))dh$$

$$= \int_y^\infty (1 - F(h))dh,$$

where the last step uses the well-known fact that $\mu = \int_0^\infty (1 - F(h))dh$. Because F's support is the positive real line, we have that $x > 0$ if $y < \infty$. Suppose $y = \infty$. Then $x = 0$ and (A3.2b) becomes

$$\int_{h^*}^\infty \frac{dF(h)}{h} = 0,$$

a contradiction. Therefore $x > 0$. ∎

4. The interval $[\max[y^L(h^*), y^R(h^*)], y^*(h^*)]$ is non-empty for every h^*.
We must show that $y^J(h^*) \leq y^*(h^*)$, for $J = L, R$. That is:

(a) $\mu \leq X_0^* + h^*$, and
(b) $x + h^* \leq X_0^* + h^*$.

Part (a) follows from the budget constraint (A3.1), which we may write:

$$X_0^* + h^* = \mu + \int_0^{h^*} (h^* - h)d\mathbf{F}(h),$$

which immediately implies part (a).

For part (b), we must show that $x \leq X_0^*$. If this were false, then X^R would give more resource to h^* than X^*, the solution to (SL2), which is impossible, which proves the claim.

5. Proof of Proposition 3.5(a)

Suppose the solution to (SL) were not the policy X^L but rather the policy $X = X^L + g$, for some non-zero function g. We know the solution must have $X(h^*) = \bar{y}$, and so we must, for a non-negative function s and non-negative number λ, define the function:

$$\Delta(\varepsilon) = \int_0^{h^*} \log(X^L(h) + \varepsilon g(h))d\mathbf{F}(h) - \int_{h_L}^{h^*} \varepsilon s(h)g'(h)dh$$

$$- \lambda\varepsilon \int_0^{h^*} g(h)d\mathbf{F}(h).$$

Note that $g' \leq 0$ on $[h_L, h^*)$ because $X'_L = 1$ on that interval; note that $\int_0^{h^*} g(h)d\mathbf{F}(h) = 0$ because g integrates to zero on the interval $[0, \infty)$, and is zero for h greater than h^*. Suppose we can find a pair (s, λ) such that Δ is maximized at $\varepsilon = 0$. Then $\Delta(0) \geq \Delta(1)$; but $\Delta(1)$ is greater than or equal to the value of the program (SL) at $X^L + g$, by construction of Δ. This contradicts the claim that X^L is not the solution to (SL).

Thus, what remains to show is that we can choose a non-negative function s on $[h_L, h^*]$ and a non-negative number λ, such that the function Δ is maximized at zero.

First, note that $\hat{X}_0^L > \hat{X}_0^R > 0$. The first inequality is obvious (from Figure 3.2). The second follows from the easy-to-see fact that $\hat{X}_0^R \geq x > 0$, where x is defined in (A3.2b). (This fact is also demonstrated in the text of Chapter 3.)

We choose:

(1) $\lambda = \frac{1}{\hat{X}_0^L}$,

(2) $s(h_L) = 0$, $s'(h) = (\lambda - \frac{1}{\hat{X}_0^L + h - h_L})f(h)$ on $[h_L, h^*)$

Note that $\lambda > 0$, and s' is clearly non-negative on its domain, so s is non-negative on its domain.

Because Δ is a concave function,[3] to show it is maximized at zero, it suffices to show that $\Delta'(0) = 0$, which we now do. Compute

---

[3] This key step is where we exploit the fact that the optimization program is concave.

that:

$$\Delta'(0) = \int_0^{h_L} \frac{g(h)f(h)}{\hat{X}_0^L} dh + \int_{h_L}^{h^*} \frac{g(h)f(h)}{\hat{X}_0^L + h - h_L} dh - \int_{h_L}^{h^*} g'(h)s(h)dh$$

$$- \lambda \left(\int_0^{h_L} g(h)f(h)dh + \int_{h_L}^{h^*} g(h)f(h)dh \right)$$

Using integration by parts to expand the term with g', and re-grouping, we have:

$$\Delta'(0) = \int_0^{h_L} \left(\frac{1}{\hat{X}_0^L} - \lambda \right) g(h)d\mathbf{F}(h)$$

$$+ \int_{h_L}^{h^*} \left[s'(h) - \left(\lambda - \frac{1}{\hat{X}_0^L + h - h_L} \right) f(h) \right] g(h)dh$$

$$- s(h^*)g(h^*) + s(h_L)g(h_L).$$

In this expression, the first term is zero by definition of λ, the second is zero by definition of s, the third term is zero because $g(h^*) = 0$, and the fourth term is zero by definition of s. This proves that X^L is the solution of (SL).

6. Proof of Proposition 3.5(b)

1. We wish to show that the function $X^R(\cdot)$, as defined in the statement of the proposition, is the solution of program (SR). Suppose to the contrary that it were not and the solution were $X^R + g$ for some non-zero function g. Then construct the function:

$$\Delta(\varepsilon) = \int_{h^*}^{\infty} \log(X^R(h) + \varepsilon g(h))d\mathbf{F}(h) + \int_0^{h^*} (1 - (X^R(h)$$

$$+ \varepsilon g'(h))) A(h)dh + \int_{h^*}^{h_R} (1 - (X^R + \varepsilon g'))C(h)dh$$

$$+ \int_{h_R}^{\infty} (X^{R'} + \varepsilon g') B(h) dh - \lambda \varepsilon \int_0^{\infty} g(h) d\mathbf{F}(h) + \rho \varepsilon g(h^*).$$

Note that $\Delta(0) = \int_{h^*}^{\infty} \log X^R(h) d\mathbf{F}(h)$. Suppose the functions A, B, and C are non-negative on their supports, as are the numbers λ and ρ. Then it follows that at the value $\varepsilon = 1$ every term in the expression for Δ is non-negative. If we can show that Δ is maximized at zero, then we will have proved the claim. As usual, because Δ is a concave function, it suffices to show that we can choose the 'Lagrangian multipliers' so that $\Delta'(0) = 0$.

2. Denote $x = \hat{X}_0^R$. We calculate, after using integration by parts and the functional form of X^R that:

$$\Delta'(0) = \int_0^{h^*} (A'(h) - \lambda f(h)) g(h) dh$$

$$+ \int_{h^*}^{h_R} \left(C'(h) + f(h) \left(\frac{1}{x+h} - \lambda \right) \right) g(h) dh$$

$$+ \int_{h_R}^{\infty} \left(f(h) \left(\frac{1}{x+h_R} - \lambda \right) - B'(h) \right) g(h) dh + g(0) A(0)$$

$$+ g(h^*)(-A(h^*) + C(h^*) + \rho) + g(h_R)(-C(h_R)$$

$$- B(h_R)) + g(\infty) B(\infty).$$

We now define:
(a) $A(0) = 0$; $A'(h) = \lambda f(h)$ on $[0, h^*]$;
(b) $C(h_R) = 0$; $C'(h) = f(h) \left(\lambda - \frac{1}{x+h} \right)$ on $[h^*, h_R]$;
(c) $\lambda = \frac{1}{x+h_R}$;
(d) $B(h) \equiv 0$;
(e) $\rho = \frac{F(h_R)}{x+h_R} - \int_{h^*}^{h^R} \frac{d\mathbf{F}(h)}{x+h}$.

We can immediately check that all the terms in the above expression for $\Delta'(0)$ vanish. The only tricky one is the coefficient of $g(h^*)$, which vanishes by calculating the values of

$A(h^*)$ and $C(h^*)$ from the definitions of their derivatives, and using the value of ρ given in (e).

It is obvious that the functions A, B, and C are non-negative on their domains and that $\lambda > 0$. Therefore, the only remaining issue is the non-negativity of ρ.

(3)   This we establish as follows. We now view the numbers x, h_R, and ρ as functions of the number $\bar{y}$ (see the statement of Proposition 3.5b). We are concerned with problems where $\bar{y} > y_R^*(h^*)$, where recall that $y_R^*(h^*) = X^R(h^*)$, and $X^R(\cdot)$ is the solution of the 'unconstrained' problem (SR1). Now we know that the value of ρ at the solution of (SR1) is zero (check Section 3 of this Appendix, and Equation (A3.2b) of that section). That is, $\rho[y_R^*(h^*)] = 0$. It therefore suffices to show that ρ is an increasing function.

We write equations (3.9c) and (3.9d) now as:

$$x(Y) + h^* = Y$$
$$x(Y) + Q(h_R(Y)) = \mu$$

where $Y = \bar{y}$ will be treated as a variable. Differentiating these equations w.r.t Y gives us:

$$x'(Y) = 1$$
$$x'(Y) + (1 - F(h_R(Y)))h'_R(Y) = 0,$$

and so compute that $1 + h'_R = \frac{-F(h_R)}{1 - F(h_R)} < 0$.

Differentiating the expression for $\rho(Y)$ from step 2, statement (e) gives – recalling that we now treat x and h_R as functions of Y – and using the fact that $x'(Y) = 1$, after some calculation:

$$\rho'(Y) = \int\limits_{h^*}^{h_R} \frac{d\mathbf{F}(h)}{(x+h)^2} - \frac{F(h_R)}{(x+h_R)^2}(1 + h'_R).$$

But we have noted earlier that $1 + h'_R < 0$, and so we have shown that $\rho'(Y) > 0$, which concludes the proof.   ∎

CHAPTER 4

7. Proof of Proposition 4.2

Part (a). Let X be a quasi-PUNE at date t. Because the mapping $h \to \alpha^t h^b r(h)^c$ is strictly monotone increasing, parents and children occupy the same ranks in their respective wage distributions, that is:

$$\forall h \quad F^{t+1}(\alpha^t h^b r(h)^c) = F^t(h) \tag{A4.1}$$

Hence, from Equation (4.2):

$$\forall h \quad \hat{F}^{t+1}\left(\frac{\mu^{t+1}}{\mu^0}\alpha^t h^b r(h)^c\right) = \hat{F}^t\left(\frac{\mu^t}{\mu^0}h\right) \tag{A4.2}$$

Let $\theta : \mathbf{R}_+ \to \mathbf{R}_+$ be defined by:

$$\forall h \in \mathbf{R}_+ \quad \frac{\mu^t}{\mu^0}h \to \frac{\mu^{t+1}}{\mu^0}\alpha^t h^b r(h)^c.$$

Then we may rewrite (A4.2) as $\hat{F}^{t+1}(h) = \hat{F}^t(\theta^{-1}(h))$, and so $\hat{F}^{t+1}(h) \gtreqless \hat{F}^t(h)$ as

$$\hat{F}^t(\theta^{-1}(h)) \gtreqless \hat{F}^t(h) \quad \text{as} \quad \theta^{-1}(h) \gtreqless h \quad \text{as} \quad h \gtreqless \theta(h)$$

$$\text{as} \quad h \gtreqless \frac{\mu^{t+1}}{\mu^t}\alpha^t h^b r(h)^c \quad \text{as} \quad \frac{h^{1-b}}{r(h)^c} \gtreqless \alpha^* \equiv \frac{\mu^{t+1}}{\mu^t}\alpha^t.$$

We next argue that the function $\zeta(h) = \frac{h^{1-b}}{r(h)^c}$ is strictly increasing on $\mathbf{R}_+$, taking on values from zero to infinity, which means that

$$(\exists h')| \, 0 \leq h < h' \Rightarrow \zeta(h) < \alpha^* \quad \text{and} \quad h > h' \Rightarrow \zeta(h) > \alpha^*.$$

This will prove part (a).

Suppose Left won the election at date t. The graph of $r(h)$ is a positive constant times the graph of X^L pictured in Figure 3.2. Obviously $\zeta(h)$ is strictly increasing on the intervals $[0, h_L)$ and $[h^*, \infty)$, where r is constant. On the interval $[h_L, h^*]$, we have $r(h) = \beta_0 + \frac{\gamma c}{1+\gamma c}h$, where $\beta_0 > 0$. Therefore on this interval

$$\zeta(h) = \frac{h^{1-b}}{\left(\beta_0 + \dfrac{\gamma c}{1 + \gamma c}h\right)^c}.$$

Therefore we have

$$\frac{d}{dh}\log\zeta(h) = \frac{1-b}{h} - \frac{\gamma c^2}{(1+\gamma c)\beta_0 + \gamma ch}.$$

and so

$$\frac{d}{dh}\log\zeta(h) > 0 \Leftrightarrow \frac{1-b}{c} > \frac{\gamma ch}{(1+\gamma c)\beta_0 + \gamma ch}.$$

Because $\beta_0 > 0$, the r.h.s. of the last inequality is smaller than unity, and hence $\zeta(h)$ is strictly increasing on $[h_L, h^*]$ if $\frac{1-b}{c} \geq 1$. But this means $b + c \leq 1$, which is our premise.

Now suppose that Right won the election at date t. Again consult Figure 3.2. Exactly the same kind of argument shows that ζ is strictly increasing.

Part (b). Because the sequence $\{\hat{F}^t\}$ is mean-preserving and $\hat{F}^{t+1}$ cuts $\hat{F}^t$ once from below, we have that $\hat{\mathbf{F}}^{t+1}$ second-order stochastic dominates $\{\hat{\mathbf{F}}^t\}$. It therefore follows that the sequence of CVs is monotone decreasing, and therefore converges.[4]   ∎

8. Proof of Theorem 4.2

1. Fix $h^* > 0$; without loss of generality, normalize by setting $h^* = 1$. At date 0, *both* parties play the policy that solves (SL2), defined in §2 of this appendix. We shall, at each date, renormalize so that the descendents of h^* always have one unit of human capital – that is, we divide all human capitals by the level of human capital of the contemporaneous member of the h^* dynasty. This does not affect coefficients of variation.

    Therefore, at date 1, denoting the human capital of the child of h by $S^1(h)$, we have:

$$S^1(h)^{\frac{1}{c}} = \frac{h^{\frac{b}{c}}(h + X_0^*)}{1(1 + X_0^*)}, \quad \text{for } h \leq 1, \tag{A4.3}$$

---

[4] We can prove that the sequence of distribution functions $\hat{F}^t$ converges weakly to a limit distribution. But all we need in what follows is the convergence of the sequence of CVs.

where X_0^* is defined by (A3.1). Equation (A4.3) follows directly from §2 of this appendix and our normalization procedure.

2. Denote the distribution of human capital at date t in the sequence $A(h^*)$ by F^t. Then we have that the total resource bundle function at date t is

$$X^t(h) = \begin{cases} X_t^* + h, & 0 \le h \le 1 \\ X_t^* + 1, & h > 1, \end{cases}$$

where X_t^* is defined by

$$X_t^* + \int_0^1 h \, dF^t(h) + (1 - F^t(1)) = \mu^t, \tag{A4.4}$$

where μ^t is the mean of distribution F^t. Thus:

$$S^2(h)^{\frac{1}{c}} = \frac{S^1(h)^{\frac{b}{c}}(S^1(h) + X_1^*)}{1 + X_1^*}, \qquad \text{for } h \le 1$$

$$= \frac{h^{\frac{b}{c}}(h + X_0^*)}{(1 + X_0^*)(1 + X_1^*)} + \frac{X_1^* S^1(h)^{\frac{b}{c}}}{1 + X_1^*},$$

using (A4.3), where $S^2(h)$ is the (normalized) human capital of the grandchild of h. By induction, for the Tth descendent we have:

$$\text{for } h \le 1, \quad S^T(h)^{\frac{1}{c}} = \frac{h^{\frac{b}{c}}(h + X_0^*)}{\prod_{j=0}^{T-1}(1 + X_j^*)} + \sum_{t=1}^{T-1} \lambda_t S^t(h)^{\frac{b}{c}}, \tag{A4.5}$$

where $\lambda_t = \frac{X_t^*}{\prod_{j=t}^{T-1}(1+X_j^*)}$, $\quad t = 1, \ldots, T-1$.

3. Let $0 < h^2 < h^1 < 1$ be two levels of human capital at date 0. If the product $\Delta = \prod_{j=0}^{\infty}(1 + X_j^*)$ converges, then from (A4.5), and the fact that $\{S^t(h) | t = 1, 2, \ldots\}$ converges, it follows that $S^\infty(h^2)^{\frac{1}{c}} < S^\infty(h^1)^{\frac{1}{c}}$, and so the CV of F^t does not converge to zero, because the ratio of human capitals of pairs of dynasties does not converge to unity.

4. Thus, to prove the claim, we need only show convergence of the infinite product Δ. Integrating by parts, note that:

$$\int_0^1 h\, dF^t(h) = F^t(1) - \int_0^1 F^t(h)\, dh,$$

and so from (A4.4) we deduce:

$$X_t^* = \int_1^\infty (1 - F^t(h))\, dh;$$

that is, X_t^* is the area 'above' the CDF on the interval $[1, \infty)$. (Use the fact that $\mu^t = \int_0^\infty (1 - F^t(h))\, dh$.) By definition of F^1 we have:

$$X_1^* = \int_1^\infty (1 - F^1(h))\, dh = \int_1^\infty (1 - F^1(S^1(h)))\, dS^1(h)$$

$$= \int_1^\infty (1 - F^0(h))\, dS^1(h),$$

because $F^0(h) = F^1(S^1(h))$ (i.e., members of a dynasty occupy the same rank in their respective distributions). For $h > 1$ we have:

$$S^1(h)^{\frac{1}{c}} = \frac{h^{\frac{b}{c}}(1 + X_0^*)}{1 + X_0^*} = h^{\frac{b}{c}},$$

and so $\frac{dS^1(h)}{dh} = bh^{b-1}$. Therefore, continuing the above expansion:

$$X_1^* = \int_1^\infty (1 - F^0(h))bh^{b-1}\, dh \leq b \int_1^\infty (1 - F^0(h))\, dh.$$

By induction, it follows that:

$$X_t^* \leq b^t \int_1^\infty (1 - F^0(h))\, dh.$$

Therefore $\sum X_t^*$ converges, because it is dominated by a converging geometric series, and, in particular, $X_t^* \to 0$. But note that

$$\log \Delta = \sum \log(1 + X_t^*),$$

which converges iff $\sum X_t^*$ converges, because for X_t^* near zero, $\log(1 + X_t^*) \cong X_t^*$. Therefore $\Delta < \infty$, as we set out to prove.

CHAPTER 5

9. Proof of Theorem 5.1

1. For this solution to be well-defined, it must be the case that $\psi^*(0) \geq 0$, which is true if and only if $y \geq h^*$, which is true if and only if premise (A1) holds.

2. Suppose that (ψ^*, r^*) were not the solution, and the solution is:

$$\psi = \psi^* + g, \quad r = r^* + q,$$

where g and q are non-zero functions on $[0, \infty)$. As in the earlier optimization proofs, we define the variation functional:

$$\Delta(\varepsilon, \beta)$$
$$= \log(\psi^*(h^*) + \varepsilon g(h^*)) + \gamma c \log(r^*(h^*) + \beta q(h^*))$$
$$+ \gamma d \log(\bar{r} + \beta \bar{q}) + \int_0^\infty R(h)\beta q'(h)dh$$
$$+ \int_0^{h^*} P(h)(1 - (\psi'(h) + \varepsilon g'(h) + 0 + \beta q'(h)))dh$$
$$+ \int_{h^*}^\infty W(h)(0 + \varepsilon g'(h))dh + \lambda(\mu - (\bar{\psi} + \varepsilon \bar{g}) - (\bar{r} + \beta \bar{q})),$$

where $\bar{g} = \int g(h)f(h)dh$, $\bar{r} = \int r(h)f(h)dh$, and $\bar{q} = \int q(h)$
$\times f(h)dh$.

Note that $\Delta(0,0)$ is the value of the objective function of the program at (ψ^*, r^*). Suppose that R, P, and W are non-negative functions on their domains, defined by the regions of integration. Note that, because (ψ, r) is in T^*, all terms in Δ are non-negative. If we can show that Δ is maximized at $(0,0)$, then it would follow that the $\Delta(0,0) \geq \Delta(1,1)$, and hence the value of the objective at (ψ^*, r^*) is at least as great as the value at $(\psi \ r)$, contradicting the claim that (ψ, r) is the solution, and thereby establishing the theorem. We note that Δ is concave, and thus, to establish that $(0,0)$ is its maximum, we need only show that its gradient is zero there.

3. First, note that (ψ, r) must be constant on the interval $[h^*, \infty)$; if these functions ever increased on that interval, we could reduce them to constants and transfer resources back to h^* and $[0, h^*)$, thus increasing the value of the objective. Therefore we must have:

$$g(h^*) = g(\infty) \quad \text{and} \quad q(h^*) = q(\infty).$$

4. We define:

$$\lambda = \frac{1}{y}, \quad P(0) = 0, \quad P'(h) = \lambda f(h) \text{ on } [0, h^*],$$

$$R(0) = 0, \quad R'(h) = \frac{\gamma d}{\bar{r}} f(h) \text{ on } [0, h^*],$$

$$R'(h) = \left(\frac{\gamma d}{\bar{r}} - \frac{1}{y} \right) f(h) \text{ on } [h^*, \infty),$$

$$W(h^*) = \frac{1 - F(h^*)}{y}, \quad W'(h) = -\lambda f(h) \text{ on } (h^*, \infty).$$

Note immediately that $W(\infty) = 0$, so $W \geq 0$ on its domain.

5. Note that

$R(h^*) = \frac{\gamma d}{\bar{r}} F(h^*)$, and so

$$R(\infty) - R(h^*) = \int_{h^*}^{\infty} R'(h)dh = \left(\frac{\gamma d}{\bar{r}} - \frac{1}{y} \right)(1 - F(h^*)).$$

Hence, to show $R(\infty) \geq 0$, we need to show that

$$R(h^*) + \left(\frac{\gamma d}{\bar{r}} - \frac{1}{y} \right)(1 - F(h^*)) \geq 0;$$

that is, that:

$$\frac{\gamma d}{\bar{r}} F(h^*) + \left(\frac{\gamma d}{\bar{r}} - \frac{1}{y}\right)(1 - F(h^*)) \geq 0.$$

But this inequality reduces to premise (A2) of the theorem. This proves that $R \geq 0$. It immediately follows that W, P, R, and λ are all non-negative.

6. We next differentiate Δ w.r.t. ε and β:

$$\frac{\partial \Delta}{\partial \varepsilon}(0, 0) = \frac{g(h^*)}{\psi(h^*)} - \int_0^{h^*} P(h)g'(h)dh + \int_{h^*}^{\infty} W(h)g'(h)dh - \lambda\bar{g},$$

$$\frac{\partial \Delta}{\partial \beta}(0, 0) = \frac{\gamma cq(h^*)}{\bar{r}} + \frac{\gamma d\bar{q}}{\bar{r}} + \int_0^{\infty} R(h)q'(h)dh$$

$$- \int_0^{h^*} P(h)q'(h)dh - \lambda\bar{q}.$$

Integrating by parts the terms with g' and r' enables us to state the claim that the derivative vanishes at the origin as:

$$0 = \frac{g(h^*)}{\psi(h^*)} + \int_0^{h^*} P'(h)g(h)dh - P(h)g(h)|_0^{h^*}$$

$$- \int_{h^*}^{\infty} W'(h)g(h)dh + W(h)g(h)|_{h^*}^{\infty} - \lambda\bar{g};$$

$$0 = \frac{\gamma cq(h^*)}{\bar{r}} + \frac{\gamma d\bar{q}}{\bar{r}} - \int_0^{\infty} R'(h)q(h)dh + R(h)q(h)|_0^{\infty}$$

$$+ \int_0^{h^*} P'(h)q(h)dh - P(h)q(h)|_0^{h^*} - \lambda\bar{q}.$$

We rewrite these two equations as:

$$0 = \frac{g(h^*)}{\psi(h^*)} - Pg|_0^{h^*} + Wg|_{h^*}^{\infty} + \int_0^{h^*} (P' - \lambda f)g(h)dh$$

$$+ \int_{h^*}^{\infty} (-W' - \lambda f)g(h)dh, \tag{A4.10}$$

$$0 = \frac{\gamma c q(h^*)}{\bar{r}} + Rq|_0^\infty - Pq|_0^{h^*}$$

$$+ \int_0^{h^*} \left(P' - R' + \left(\frac{\gamma d}{\bar{r}} - \lambda \right) f \right) q(h) dh$$

$$+ \int_{h^*}^\infty \left(-R' + \left(\frac{\gamma d}{\bar{r}} - \lambda \right) f \right) q(h) dh. \qquad \text{(A4.11)}$$

The four terms with integrals in these equations vanish, by definition of the functions P, R, and W (see step 3). Hence, to verify Equations (A4.10) and (A4.11), we need only verify that the endpoint terms vanish.

Those endpoint terms in Equation (A4.10) will vanish if:

$$\frac{1}{\psi^*(h^*)} - P(h^*) - W(h^*) = 0 \text{ (coefficient of } g(h^*))$$

$P(0) = 0$ (coefficient of $g(0)$)
$W(\infty) = 0$ (coefficient of $g(\infty)$)

We have already established the second and third lines; the first line reduces to $\frac{1}{y} = \lambda F(h^*) + \lambda(1 - F(h^*)) = \lambda$, which is true.

The endpoint conditions in Equation (A4.11) will vanish if:

$$\frac{\gamma c}{\bar{r}} + R(\infty) - P(h^*) = 0 \quad \text{(coefficientof } q(h^*))$$
$$-R(0) + P(0) = 0 \quad \text{(coefficient of } q(0)).$$

The second line is obviously true. To verify the first line, note that $R(\infty) = \frac{\gamma d}{\bar{r}} - \frac{1 - F(h^*)}{y}$ and $P(h^*) = \frac{F(h^*)}{y}$. Substituting into the first line above, we reduce it to showing that $\bar{r} = \gamma(c + d)y$, which is true by definition, and the theorem is established. ∎

10. Proof of Theorem 5.2

1. We first establish that the solution is well-defined, which means that there is a unique solution (r_0, h_1) with r_0 positive and $0 < h_1 < h^*$. We have already observed that r_0 is positive. For the second claim, evaluate equation (b) at $h_1 = 0$, and note that the l.h.s. of (b) is less than the r.h.s. by invoking premise (B1). As h_1 increases from zero to h^*, the l.h.s. increases monotonically

to infinity, and the r.h.s. decreases monotonically to a finite number. (One observes this by differentiating the r.h.s. with respect to h_1.) Therefore, a unique solution, h_1, to (B3b) exists, given (B3a). Therefore (ψ^*, r^*) is well-defined.

2. As usual in these proofs, assume that the solution is indeed

$$\psi = \psi^* + g, \quad r = r^* + q,$$

for some non-zero functions g and q. We remark, as in the previous theorem, that $g(h^*) = g(\infty)$ and $q(h^*) = q(\infty)$. Define the function:

$$\Delta(\varepsilon, \beta) = \log(h^* - h_1 + \varepsilon g(h^*)) + \gamma c \log(r_0 + h_1 + \beta q(h^*))$$

$$+ \gamma d \log(r_0 + Q(h_1) + \beta \bar{q}) + \int_0^{h_1} (0 + \varepsilon g(h)) S(h) dh$$

$$+ \int_0^{h^*} (1 - (\psi'(h) + \varepsilon g'(h) + r'(h) + \beta q'(h))) V(h) dh$$

$$+ \int_{h^*}^{\infty} \varepsilon g'(h) T(h) dh$$

$$+ \int_{h_1}^{\infty} \beta q'(h) W(h) dh + \lambda(\mu - (\bar{\psi} + \varepsilon \bar{g}) - (\bar{r} + \beta \bar{q})).$$

Note that Δ is concave, and that $\Delta(0, 0)$ is the utility of type h^* at the policy (ψ^*, r^*), because all the integral terms vanish. We will display non-negative functions S, V, T, and W, and a non-negative number λ, for which the function Δ is maximized at $(0, 0)$, which will contradict the claim that (ψ, r) dominates (ψ^*, r^*).

3. The derivatives of Δ at the origin are:

$$\frac{\partial \Delta}{\partial \varepsilon}(0, 0) = \frac{g(h^*)}{h^* - h_1} + \int_0^{h_1} g(h) S(h) dh - \int_0^{h^*} g'(h) V(h) dh$$

$$+ \int_{h^*}^{\infty} g'(h) T(h) dh - \lambda \bar{g},$$

$$\frac{\partial \Delta}{\partial \beta}(0,0) = \frac{\gamma c q(h^*)}{r_0 + h_1} + \frac{\gamma d \bar{q}}{r_0 + Q(h_1)} - \int_0^{h^*} q'(h)V(h)dh$$

$$+ \int_{h_1}^{\infty} q'(h)W(h)dh - \lambda \bar{q}.$$

Integrating by parts, we write the statement that these derivatives are zero as:

$$0 = \frac{g(h^*)}{h^* - h_1} + \int_0^{h_1} g(h)S(h) - g(h)V(h)|_0^{h^*} + \int_0^{h^*} g(h)V'(h)dh$$

$$+ g(h)T(h)|_{h^*}^{\infty} - \int_{h^*}^{\infty} g(h)T'(h)dh - \lambda \int_0^{\infty} g(h)f(h)dh,$$

$$(A4.12)$$

$$0 = \frac{\gamma c q(h^*)}{r_0 + h_1} + \bar{q}\left(\frac{\gamma d}{r_0 + Q(h_1)} - \lambda\right) - q(h)V(h)|_0^{h^*}$$

$$+ \int_0^{h^*} q(h)V'(h)dh + q(h)W(h)|_{h_1}^{\infty} - \int_{h_1}^{\infty} q(h)W'(h)dh.$$

$$(A4.13)$$

4. To annihilate all the terms in Equation (A4.12), we require:

(1a) $\frac{1}{h^* - h_1} - V(h^*) + T(\infty) - T(h^*) = 0$ (coefficient of $g(h^*)$ and $g(\infty)$);

(1b) $V(0) = 0$ (coefficient of $g(0)$)

(1c) $S(h) + V'(h) - \lambda f(h) = 0$ on $[0, h_1]$;

(1d) $V'(h) = \lambda f(h)$ on $[h_1, h^*]$;

(1e) $-T'(h) - \lambda f(h) = 0$ on $[h^*, \infty)$.

To annihilate all the terms in Equation (A4.13), we require:

(2a) $\frac{\gamma c}{r_0 + h_1} - V(h^*) + W(\infty) = 0$ (coefficient of $q(h^*)$ and $q(\infty)$);

(2b) $V(0) = 0$ (coefficient of $q(0)$);

(2c) $W(h_1) = 0$ (coefficient of $q(h_1)$);

(2d) $V'(h) = \left(\lambda - \frac{\gamma d}{r_0 + Q(h_1)}\right) f(h)$ on $[0, h_1]$;

(2e) $V'(h) - W'(h) = \left(\lambda - \frac{\gamma d}{r_0 + Q(h_1)}\right) f(h)$ on $[h_1, h^*]$;

(2f) $W'(h) = \left(\frac{\gamma d}{r_0 + Q(h_1)} - \lambda\right) f(h)$ on $[h^*, \infty)$.

(5) We construct non-negative functions to satisfy these ten equations as follows. Equations (2b) and (2d) define V on $[0, h_1]$. Equation (1d) defines V on $[h_1, h^*]$. Then Equation (1c) defines S as

$$S(h) = \frac{\gamma d f(h)}{r_0 + Q(h_1)} \text{ on } [0, h_1].$$

Integrating V' on the interval $[0, h^*]$ produces:

$$V(h^*) = \lambda F(h^*) - \frac{\gamma d F(h_1)}{r_0 + Q(h_1)}.$$

Equation (1e) tells us that

$$T(\infty) - T(h^*) = -\lambda(1 - F(h^*)),$$

and so, substituting the last two equations into (1a), we define λ as:

$$\lambda = \frac{1}{h^* - h_1} + \frac{\gamma d F(h_1)}{r_0 + Q(h_1)}.$$

We note immediately from Equation (B3b) in the statement of the theorem that λ is positive. We have now exhausted the information in (1a)–(1e).

Equation (2a) now says that

$$W(\infty) = \lambda F(h^*) - \frac{\gamma d F(h_1)}{r_0 + Q(h_1)} - \frac{\gamma c}{r_0 + h_1};$$

Equation (2e) says that:

$$W'(h) = \frac{\gamma d}{r_0 + Q(h_1)} f(h) \text{ on } [h_1, h^*].$$

Integrating:

$$W(\infty) - W(h_1) = \int_{h_1}^{h^*} W' \, dh + \int_{h^*}^{\infty} W' \, dh$$

$$= \frac{\gamma d}{r_0 + Q(h_1)}(F(h^*) - F(h_1))$$

$$+ \left(\frac{\gamma d}{r_0 + Q(h_1)} - \lambda\right)(1 - F(h^*)), \text{ using (2f).}$$

Defining $W(h_1) = 0$ (see Equation (2c)), we thus have two expressions for $W(\infty)$. Consistency requires they be equal. Indeed, their equality follows exactly from Equation (B3b) in the statement of the theorem.

What remains to be checked is the non-negativity of the functions V, S, T, and W. S is fine. For V to be increasing on $[0, h_1]$ requires $\lambda > \frac{\gamma d}{r_0 + Q(h_1)}$, which is true by definition of λ and Equation (b) of the statement. V is obviously increasing on $[h_1, h^*]$. We are at liberty to set $T(\infty) = 0$, and it then follows from our specification of T' (see (1(e)) that T is non-negative on its domain. Only W is left, which is non-negative on its domain if $W(\infty) \geq 0$, that is, if:

$$\lambda F(h^*) \geq \frac{\gamma d}{r_0 + Q(h_1)} F(h_1) + \frac{\gamma c}{r_0 + h_1}.$$

By substituting in our value of λ, and using Equation (b) of the statement, this inequality reduces to premise (B2). ∎

11. Proof of Theorem 5.3

1. We shall normalize the distributions at each date to maintain h^* and all its descendents at $h^{*t} = 1$. We study the dynamic process of investment, where the investment equation at date t is defined by Theorem 5.2 and the time-dated parameters (r_0^t, h_1^t) are given by:

   (B3a^t) $r_0^t = \mu^t - Q^t(1)$,

   (B3b^t) $\frac{1}{1-h_1^t} = \frac{\gamma c}{r_0^t + h_1^t} + \frac{\gamma d(1 - F^t(h_1^t))}{r_0^t + Q^t(h_1^t)}.$

2. The human capital of the child of h, given the normalization, which requires dividing all children's human capital by the human capital of the child of $h^* = 1$, is:

$$S(h) = \begin{cases} h^b \left(\dfrac{r_0 + h}{r_0 + h_1} \right)^{1-b}, & \text{if } h < h_1 \\ h^b, & \text{if } h \geq h_1. \end{cases}$$

3. We first show that $r_0^t \to 0$.

$$r_0^t = \mu^t - Q^t(1) = \int_1^\infty h d\mathbf{F}^t(h) - (1 - F^t(1))$$

$$= \int_1^\infty (h - 1)d\mathbf{F}^t(h);$$

but $\int_1^\infty h d\mathbf{F}^t(h) = \int_1^\infty h^{b^t} d\mathbf{F}^0(h)$, by step 2, and so

$$r_0^t = \int_1^\infty (h^{b^t} - 1)d\mathbf{F}^0(h).$$

Let $\varepsilon > 0$ be given, and choose $H > 1$ such that

$$\int_H^\infty (h - 1)d\mathbf{F}^0(h) < \frac{\varepsilon}{2}.$$

Further, choose a date T such that

$$H^{b^T} - 1 < \frac{\varepsilon}{2(1 - F^0(H))}.$$

Then

$$r_0^T = \int_1^H (h^{b^T} - 1)d\mathbf{F}^0(h) + \int_H^\infty (h^{b^T} - 1)d\mathbf{F}^0(h)$$

$$< (H^{b^T} - 1)(1 - F^0(H)) + \int_H^\infty (h - 1)d\mathbf{F}^0(h)$$

$$< \frac{\varepsilon}{2(1 - F^0(H))}(1 - F^0(H)) + \frac{\varepsilon}{2} = \varepsilon.$$

It follows that $r_0^t \to 0$.

4. Because $Q^t(h_1^t) = \int_0^{h_1^t} h d\mathbf{F}^t(h) + h_1^t(1 - F^t(h_1^t))$, we may rewrite Equation (B3b^t) as:

    $$\frac{1}{1 - h_1^t} = \frac{\gamma c}{r_0^t + h_1^t} + \frac{\gamma d}{R^t + h_1^t},$$

    where $R^t = \frac{r_0^t}{1 - F^t(h_1^t)} + \frac{1}{1 - F^t(h_1^t)} \int_0^{h_1^t} h d\mathbf{F}^t(h)$.

    Let $\hat{h}$ be a positive limit point of $\{h_1^t\}$ and denote a convergent subsequence again by $\{h_1^t\}$. Let $\hat{R} = \lim R^t$. Then, using the fact that $r_0^t \to 0$, the limit point must satisfy the equation:

    $$\frac{1}{1 - \hat{h}} = \frac{\gamma c}{\hat{h}} + \frac{\gamma d}{\hat{R} + \hat{h}}. \tag{A3.14}$$

    Solving this equation for $\hat{h}$, while viewing $\hat{R}$ as a parameter, we see:

    (i) $\hat{h} = \frac{\gamma(c+d)}{1 + \gamma(c+d)}$, if $\hat{R} = 0$,

    (ii) $\hat{h}$ is a decreasing function of $\hat{R}$.

    It thus follows that all positive limit points of $\{h_1^t\}$ are no larger than $\frac{\gamma(c+d)}{1 + \gamma(c+d)}$: in particular, one is not a limit point.

    Note, as well, by inspection of Equation (A4.14), that the limit points of $\{h_1^t\}$ are bounded away from zero.

5. Because, with the normalization of step 1, the distributions $\{F^t\}$ are converging, it follows that there is a unique limit point of $\{h_1^t\}$; call it $\hat{h}$.

6. Because $r_0^t \to 0$ and the limit point of $\{h_1^t\}$ is positive, we may write an approximation to $S(h)$ for large t as (consult the formula of step 2):

    $$S(h) = \begin{cases} \dfrac{h}{(h_1^t)^{1-b}}, & \text{if } h < h_1^t \\ h^b, & \text{if } h \geq h_1^t \end{cases}.$$

    In particular, we have $S(h) > h$ always for large t.

7. Suppose there is an h at date 0, such that, for an infinite number of dates t, $S^t(h) < h_1^t$. Then, by step 6, for large t, we can write to a good approximation: $S^{t+1}(h) = \frac{S^t(h)}{h^{1-b}}$. Because this inequality holds for an infinite sequence of dates, and $S^t(h)$ is increasing in

t for large t, it follows that $S^{t+1}(h)$ increases without bound (as we are periodically dividing by the number $\hat{h}^{1-b}$, which is less than 1). But this contradicts the assumption that $S^t(h) < h_1^t$ an infinite number of times.

8. Therefore, for any positive h at date 0, eventually all his or her descendents (at large t) have human capital at least h_1^t. Because the rank $F^t(S^t(h))$ is constant, this implies that $\lim F^t(h_1^t) = 0$. Consequently, the descendents of every positive Eve are eventually in the region where investment is a constant, and the CVH converges to zero.

9. From the formula for R^t in step 4, it follows that $\lim R^t = 0$, and hence that $\hat{h} = \frac{\gamma(c+d)}{1+\gamma(c+d)}$. ∎

Index

Other titles in the series *(continued from page iii)*